# GETTING IN

## A Guide to Acceptance
## at the College of Your Choice

# GETTING IN

## A GUIDE TO ACCEPTANCE AT THE COLLEGE OF YOUR CHOICE

Random House

**NEW YORK**

First Printing

Copyright © 1972 by Joel Levine and
Lawrence May

All rights reserved under International
and Pan-American Copyright Conven-
tions. Published in the United States by
Random House, Inc., New York, and
simultaneously in Canada by Random
House of Canada Limited, Toronto.

Library of Congress Cataloging in Publication Data
Levine, Joel.
    Getting in.
    SUMMARY: Advises high school students on the most
likely methods of being accepted at the college of their
choice.
    1. Universities and colleges—United States—Ad-
mission. 2. Universities and colleges—United States—
Entrance requirements. [1. Universities and colleges—
Admission] I. May, Lawrence, joint author. II. Title.
LB2351.L4          378.1'05'60973          72–2001
ISBN 0–394–47880–0 (hardbound)
ISBN 0–394–70785–0 (paperbound)

Manufactured in the United States
of America
by American Book–Stratford Press, Inc.,
New York

For
*Gertie and Bernie*
*Harry and Edie*
Our Parents

# Acknowledgments

The authors wish to express their deepest appreciation to the deans of admissions, members of college admissions committees and the guidance counselors who furnished so much of the practical advice on how to get into college.

We wish to thank those who contributed to this book who, due to the confidential nature of their position or the sensitive nature of their experience, wish to remain anonymous.

Thanks to the hundreds of college students throughout the country who shared a few hours with us. And special thanks to Margo May (Vassar '73), Larry's sister, for her emergency treks to Cambridge and New York City, her research and her tireless assistance in typing draft after draft, rewrite after rewrite, at 3 A.M., after 3 A.M.

To Andrew Tobias (Harvard '68, Harvard Bus. '72), who helped us prepare the "Money" chapter, and to Michael Barrett, who helped us with the College Boards chapter.

And to: Mary Newburger (Radcliffe '67, N.Y.U. Med. '73); Dan Feldman (Columbia '70, Harvard Law '73); Judy Willis (Williams '71, UCLA Med. '75); Marc Drucker (Columbia '69, Harvard Bus. '71); Sara Nathan (Trinity '75) and her boyfriend Mike (University of Pennsylvania '75); Susan Landon (Simmons '71); Richard Rodwin, Harvard Club School's Committee; Gladys Bernstein, teacher and guidance counselor at Midwood High School, Brooklyn, N.Y.; Harley Lewin (Wisconsin '66 and Wisconsin Law '69); Irwin Tenenbaum (University of Pennsylvania '61 and Penn Law '64); John (Cornell), Gordon (Harvard), Lew (Harvard), Dan (Yale), Russ (Princeton) and Jon (Harvard) who helped Larry through medical school while he was writing this book; Marilyn (Bradley '74), Joel's sister, who had nothing to do with this book but would have been the only member of our families not acknowledged; and Rebecca, Joel's phenomenal wife, despite whom, and with whose help, this book was written.

And to the many friends and acquaintances who related an experience, gave us a suggestion or lead; and finally to the eight million people who play the college admissions game for real stakes.

Thank you, thank you, thank you,
Joel and Larry

# Contents

# GETTING IN

A Guide to Acceptance
at the College of Your Choice

# I
## The
## Admissions
## Process

Some years ago a monkey was accepted into the freshman class of a prestigious university. In another celebrated case, Princeton recently welcomed a Mr. Orez, apparently not having noticed that Orez is Zero spelled backward. Several undergraduates had fabricated Mr. Orez's credentials by taking his boards, forging a transcript, writing recommendations and appearing in his place at the college interview. These perceptive Princetonians demonstrated that the presentation of credentials was, in that situation, more important in college admissions than even the existence of an applicant. While such examples are extreme, they do show that the system by which high school students are accepted into colleges *can* be manipulated.

The college admissions process is often criticized as inhuman and arbitrary, but in many ways it is less arbitrary than much of life. Our very existence is the result of a chance union between two of billions of cells produced by two of billions of people. Our basic endowments of intellect, appearance, coordination and personality develop from a peculiar confluence of heredity and environment largely beyond our control. Our place of birth and beginning station in life, the lasting attitudes we pick up before age four, the draft lottery—these are some of the determining life experiences forced on us by destiny.

Yet, in the game of college admissions you need not be a helpless seed, freely blown by the winds of fate. You are a person with subtle dimensions of intellect, imagination and ingenuity, and you can influence acceptance by the college you want to attend. You can choose a school from the twenty-three hundred options available and help determine your acceptance by your own efforts. There is no single trick that will guarantee admission to college. There are many tricks. This book will explore a philosophy, a method and an approach which will equip you to meet the barrage of examinations, applications and interviews.

## To College or Not to College

As your eyes drift to the clock in your high school English class for the sixth time in as many minutes, Mrs. Rorshack is mercilessly boring you with her interpretation of "The Wilting Daffodil." Miss Gilbert gave you a bad X for talking in third-year French and Mr. Hockshtup reprimanded you for not doing your two-hour math assignment. Why do you take all this abuse? Why are you stifling your creativity, muzzling your mind and repressing your rampant sex drive? Why? Because you want to go to college, and high school is the primary prerequisite for admission.

**Negative**

From time to time, and especially once the application hassle begins, you may be tempted to completely reject the notion of college. You may think the drivel prescribed during your twelve years of early schooling was trivial and irrelevant and the prospect of advanced drivel seems singularly unappealing.

You may perceive that college-educated leaders have not spared this country recurrent wars, economic crises, internal strife, bitterness, prejudice, a deterioration of the environment, and the burden of our collective stupidity. Furthermore, there is an increasing suspicion in certain quarters that the opportunities for growth may be greater outside, in the real world, rather than within the hallowed walls of the universities. Why be restricted to the nine books that one professor believes represent the cumulative wisdom of Western thought? The ideas one explores in college are not its exclusive domain; the books, the music and the art of our civilization are all available without the payment of tuition fees.

The economic value of a degree has also been questioned. College-educated cabdrivers, waitresses, dishwashers, secretaries and infantry soldiers demonstrate that a college education is no longer the guarantee of economic security and social success it was once considered. (That is, for those sheepskin-holders who aren't cabdrivers, waitresses, dishwashers, secretaries and infantry soldiers because they want to be.)

Even if a college degree is a stepping stone to professionalism, is it worth it? If one cynically views scholars as pedants pondering footnotes in obscure and long-forgotten works, lawyers as guardians of the fortunes of the rich, and physicians as dispensers of diet pills, tranquilizers and paternalism, it is difficult to justify an irrelevant eight-year trek down the academic path. Finally, how can you spend time indulging a penchant for poetry when the streets remain filthy, the air unbreathable? While the poor get poorer, the sick die, and the country suffers from a pandemic spiritual malaise? It's easy. It's worthwhile. We recommend it.

### Positive

The university may be a tool of the system, underwritten by the society it was established to serve, but it can also serve as the source of society's transcendence. While colleges do turn out cogs for the societal machine, they also cultivate the prophets of new truths. We can use these institutions to prepare ourselves to articulate and constructively challenge the limitations of the past.

You can't do a damn thing for anybody if you don't know anything. Academic rigor may have its problems, but technical skills are indispensable for building schools or hospitals, designing mass transportation, controlling pollution, caring for physical and emotional ills, protecting civil liberties and expanding the limits of man's knowledge.

Without knowledge and ability, a burning passion to serve humanity is nothing more than a private ego trip. A Friends Service volunteer in Pakistan is a useless well-wisher unless he has the skill to rebuild a village. Ghetto businessmen are not interested in VISTA volunteers who do not understand accounting or marketing.

Changing the world takes more than passionate polemic. Among other things—like plain dumb luck—it takes a lot of technical skill and a broad foundation of knowledge.

Aside from the public good, there is great potential for personal devolopment at most colleges. Think of college as a gift of four societally sanctioned years to indulge your curiosities, explore all sorts of ideas, and find out who you are and who you'd like to be. All this can be done without the numbing pressures of having to show up at some job every day—and work. College, despite the grind, does give you an incredible amount of free time and facilities for growth and pleasure.

Most colleges have great libraries, good theater, prominent lectures, art exhibitions, cheap movies, elaborate athletic facilities, wild parties, and people to play and sleep with. You'll have the chance to make friends who share your problems and your views, yet who have perspectives that are different from yours. People have time to discuss each other, books, current events and sex. After college, when you meet new people, they are often on the opposite side of the bargaining table, on the same rung of the competitive ladder, or on their way to two different appointments. Relationships at college grow while you live, eat and study together, and they often become friendships that can have meaning for your whole life.

Just because high school bored you, it doesn't follow that college will. In fact, there's a long history of people who, after a completely turned-off high school career, have become excited by intellectual matters when they reached college. Defensive educators explain that these individuals are "late bloomers," but a better bet is that they never had a creative idea put to them before. There are interesting, enormously erudite, eccentric, active people on university faculties. Once you get into college, make sure you take their courses.

College is a further improvement on high school in the sheer variety of its academic possibilities. In most colleges these days, you are not locked into the traditional, limited curriculum that most high schools recycle for the eighty-third year and then force upon you. For example, if you choose the right school, you can take Sanskrit, Baroque music, the Politics of the Street or whatever else turns you on.

In fact, college may be the first—and sometimes, sadly, the last—opportunity you will have to learn the things you want to know from people who can tell you.

It is true that a college education is not an assurance of material success. The degree no longer opens every door. But the absence of such formal certification may keep closed certain doors you really want to go through. If you're into status, in our status-conscious culture, you will find college is a useful social credential. Dating a Yale man or a Vassar woman (or a Yale woman or a Vassar man) is the sophisticated version of "I'm going out with a 427 Corvette." Although this is one of our less than endearing realities, it would be naïve not to recognize its existence. If you care about such things, you're dead without a degree.

If you hate the idea of college because it is cloistered, live off-campus. Live in the ghetto, and break bread with the people. Going to college isn't necessarily synonymous with copping out for four years. In a fundamental sense, it is your job for those years and it does not preclude social involvement. Young people need tutors, poor people need health education. Streets need cleaning. You're young. You can do these things and study to do them better at the same time.

### A Degree of Choice

You may be one of those people who are dying to go to college and who feel no social or family pressure at all; or you may be backing into a university as the line of least resistance. In any event, you are going—or you want to. Now what?

## *The Mission*

Your job now is to think, plan, and attempt to maximize your chances for college admission without destroying your life.

One way to prepare is to get straight A's in high school. You can grind, grind, grind; use every available minute to study; eat rapidly; sleep fully clothed so as not to waste time dressing and undressing; and spend Saturday night monastically hunched over an algebra text. You can be burdened by an overloaded schedule of difficult courses, so that no subject is studied adequately. You can be concerned that you have as many honor classes as Joe, as high grades as Mary, and as many activities as Felix. While this approach might result (it might not) in acceptance by some school, you have needlessly cheated yourself out of four years of life. High school is a time to live and explore. Many good colleges value "well-roundedness" and would gladly sacrifice a few grade points for a well-developed individual. The real winner in that trade-off is you.

There is another, reverse approach to the high school experience. You need not be hassled by attendance requirements, homework assignments and test dates. You can punt, punt, punt. Take the easiest courses and do the minimum to pass; cut a maximum amount of the time; and constantly challenge your teacher's authority on principle. Turn on before class, split after lunch and indulge all of your fantasies on the teacher's time. Expose incompetence, confront injustice and speak your mind. This hedonistic approach, while perhaps more attractive than grinding, practically insures that the college option will be closed to you.

Learning does not exclude enjoying life. If you have an intellectual interest, develop it. It could even turn out to be fun. Use good teachers to go beyond requirements, and bad ones to maximize free time. Even daydreams can be creative. Experiment with sports, with new ideas, new philosophies, new cultures, music, art, and the community around you. You'll probably have a good time, and when you get to the college sweepstakes you'll find that admissions committees will be pleased at the diversity of your interests.

Colleges are not looking for academic machines. What they want are human beings of different persuasions who will benefit from education and contribute to the academic community. Though grades are important, most schools look beyond the numbers and the gold stars in admitting students. You, as an applicant, must help the college see your good qualities. You are going to have to think of yourself, during the coming ordeal, not as the unfettered and free spirit you are, but as a Really Interesting Candidate to present to the admissions committee.

## Grades—The Mark of Acceptance

Grades are not the *sine qua non* of acceptance, but they can be very, very helpful. If you have the option of getting good grades, get them.

Don't fall behind in your courses. Learn to cram productively. Think about how to take exams successfully. Write your papers in good time utilizing the best sources and help available to you.

You may be telling yourself that it's too late for this advice. Your grades may already be on record, but, it probably is true that the marks you get in your junior year are inordinately important and you should try to salvage what you can. Colleges tend to make allowances for bad grades in your freshman year and by the time you're a senior they're already making their judgment.

Speaking of teachers, grades all too often represent the subjective judgment of your teacher and it may be wise to occasionally substitute his interpretation of reality for the truth as you see it. It isn't really necessary to remind your teachers every day that "Those who can, do, and those who can't, teach." And while we're about it, stop telling doddering Mrs. Simpson that Sinclair Lewis is not a contemporary social critic. Console yourself in the knowledge that a teacher's authority over you is temporary, but be cautious while he's still in control.

### Courses—Subject to Interests

There is a famous Cambridge supermarket story about a young man, bespectacled in wire rims, unloading his overflowing shopping cart on the express counter. The burly manager, with forefinger extended in the direction of a sign, EXPRESS LINE—10 ITEMS OR LESS, looked demandingly at our friend and said, "OK, kid, which is it? You go to MIT and you can't read or you go to Harvard and can't count?"

Even the most selective colleges don't expect everyone to excel in everything. Get preparation in academic fundamentals and develop your own strong point, but do not stretch for advanced placement French if you're a language moron, or take college-level physics if you think "moments of force" are something you see in war movies.

A satisfying course of action, for your own life as well as for the college admissions game, is to do what you like and distinguish yourself in that area. In your strong subjects, take the advanced placement course. Create opportunities to shine in your high school. Initiate clubs, seminars and independent projects in the area of your interest. Investigate the possibilities for taking courses at local colleges. If there is something you enjoy doing in school, on the athletic field, in the library, in the ghetto, in the lab, or in your room— do it!

### Extracurricular—Nobody Wants a Dilettante

Colleges prefer singular achievement to plural sheeplike participation. Membership on the mimeograph squad is not likely to influence the disposition of your college application.

If you spread yourself too thin, the admissions boards aren't going to be able to latch onto "what-type-person" you are. It is much better if you are specialized so they can remember: "Oh, yeah, that's the kid who's the chess nut— good man." It's also much better for you to spend your free time doing what you enjoy.

If government turns you on, try for the Student Council. Whether it is an impotent clique of spineless wimps or a group of leaders of the people hamstrung by a narrow-minded administration, you can learn from experience how group organizations use and waste time. Knowing directly from experience is usually better than knowing from some other way.

If science is your passion, find a science teacher in your school who is willing to direct you to research and to science competitions like the Westinghouse or the City Science Fair. You'll probably enjoy it, and certainly it's the kind of "serious commitment" that impresses admissions committees.

Start a rock group, work in volunteer activities, make a film, write a poem, climb a mountain or hike across Brazil. Do what you want to do, and when the time comes, phrase it well on your college application and talk right up during your interview.

### Athletics—Admissions Are Better with a Varsity Letter

Athletics assume importance beyond "developing co-operativeness, team spirit, discipline, perseverance and an appreciation of good competition." The athlete is inextricably tied to our ideal of American virility. Alumni donations, for better or worse, are still influenced by a winning football team. Athletes are still preferentially admitted, given scholarships, and accorded a deference well beyond what their intellectual gifts might merit.

Even if you're five foot four, 120 pounds, and not likely to lead your college to the Rose Bowl, the admissions committee will appreciate your gutsiness and courage. You could choose a less threatening sport or one that isn't widely played, like fencing, and organize a team. It will demonstrate initiative, and make you appear well rounded. You could even be a starter.

If you're a good athlete, pick your best sport and develop yourself into a varsity prospect. One sport with real potential for intercollegiate competition is worth a dozen high school varsity letters.

For the athletically minded who have an interest in international relations, it may be noted that Ping-Pong is gaining in popularity.

### Community Participation—Give a Damn

Do you care about people? Be part of the solution whether or not you go to college. There are students in your own school who need tutoring and little kids in your neighborhood who would love a big brother or sister. Friends and acquaintances are getting hooked on drugs and need help. If it's clear you've got a social conscience and do something about it, any college you'd want to go to should be pleased, and any college that would look down on this kind of activity you wouldn't want anyway.

**Vacation—What to Do When School's Through**

Summer vacation may be a time out from high school routine, but you can still use it to score points in the admissions game. Several boarding schools and many colleges offer excellent summer programs. The National Science Foundation sponsors a number of summer science institutes at various universities. If you are bored by a pedestrian high school curriculum, you're in for a surprise, because, in many of these summer programs, courses as diverse as Swahili, quantum chemistry and philosophy of education are available. Further, for one whose social life has been inhibited by curfews and parental shadows, coed residence at a secluded campus offers intriguing possibilities.

Aside from what you'll get out of it, colleges looking for evidence of academic interest may be impressed that you've sought a demanding program on your own initiative.

*Employment*

If you're under thirty or over forty, it's practically impossible to find a job at all. As for summer jobs, or part-time jobs for high school students, the subject is almost too painful to mention.

However, don't despair. Initiate. There's a real lack of personal service in our egalitarian society, and youth can become the new immigrant class in America. Establish a cleaning service for homes, stores, offices, garages or attics. Pick up mail and newspapers for people who are on vacation. Walk dogs, pull weeds, mow lawns, landscape, wash cars, baby-sit, or start a neighborhood day-care center.

This kind of Horatio Algerism results in bread, experience, and incidentally can't hurt your college credentials.

*Travel*

If you're lucky enough to be able to travel and can benefit personally and culturally from this experience, that will help. In fact, this is what the entire process is all about—demonstrating that you will do well in an academic situation by showing that you can wring dry the things you're involved in already.

## Be Different

Colleges are faced with admitting the fortunate few from the qualified many. "Interesting" people with "exceptional" achievements, or those who can make themselves look that way, stand a much better chance of surviving the sifter. Hobbies like speleology are better than stamp collecting. Pets like falcons are better than dogs. Raising money for an Asian disaster area is better than raising money for the Heart Fund. A solo ballet recital is better than a bowling trophy. Colleges love to get one of a kind, and nothing would please a dean more than to be able to welcome a freshman class which boasted 44 valedictorians, 28 Merit Scholars, 47 school newspaper editors, 39 Student Council presidents, a former Green Beret, a rehabilitated armed robber and a female Olympic discus thrower.

## The Shell Game

The four years of high school are four years out of your short life. Don't take getting into college so seriously that you fall into the trap of thinking of these years exclusively as a time to prepare for college. Some of the people around you would be only too happy to turn you into a plastic shell, a sycophant, hungrily scavenging for good grades and participating in all the right activities.

The next step would be a repetition of the pattern in college—the right courses, the grade point, and the strained but proper extracurricular participation—all designed to get you into the right graduate school. Then, the right graduate school becomes preparation for the right job, and all is preparation for a life in the right neighborhood, with the right friends, proper prestige and secure security.

Don't get tricked into leading a preparatory life in the blind pursuit of means to ends which turn out to be means to some other end you never wanted in the first place. This approach isn't even necessary to get where you want to go—especially, as you're about to learn, in the case of college.

# II

# Select,
# Don't Settle

College can be endless weeks of cruel pressure, exams, papers and grades; an uninterrupted drug stupor, sex orgy, beer blast, bull session; an escape, a four-year moratorium on decision—but it is more likely to be a profound intellectual, social and emotional experience that will affect your idea of yourself, your choice of friends and mate, and what you will be and do in this incarnation. College experiences are as different as the twenty-three hundred colleges and eight million students who attend them.

You can't realistically hope to examine all the colleges that might suit your needs, but you can get straight a few considerations that are important to you, and begin to see the types of school you want and a way to get there.

## The School's Reputation

If admission is assured to anyone who can pay tuition, a school is not likely to have a strong academic reputation. One college in Iowa, notorious for accepting all comers, periodically loses and regains its accreditation as the number of volumes in its library fluctuates. This type of college should be avoided if you want a decent education. If you plan to transfer without any credits, or merely to hang loose, you might consider such an unstable school.

Unequivocally, you should go to the best school you can. This sounds cold and pragmatic, but we live in a competitive world. Most young people have pleasant personalities and we all think we are charming, but graduate schools and employers want more. When you look for that perfect first job, your school's reputation can be decisive. In many cases, talent eventually wins out: an editor from City College can work in a carpeted office alongside her Ivy League colleagues, and a systems analyst from Bentley might match the earnings of an MIT graduate. But the fight for the first job is tough when you're stuck reading the want ads or when you're forced to start rungs lower because no one has heard of Oglethorpe University. While it is pompous, it is of undeniable value to say, "I was educated at Yale."

Many schools are now adopting pass-fail grading systems and some are abandoning grades altogether. However, colleges themselves are rated by graduate schools and prospective employers. No longer available is the great equalizer of grades: "I have an A average from Getchorgoomy University." With pass-fail grading, a tremendous student at a not-so-tremendous school has less opportunity to be impressive. Your initial choice of school can therefore be more vital to your future than all four years of performance.

How do you judge reputation? By the number of graduates in *Who's Who?* Recognition by your mother's bridge club? The offer of blind dates by status-conscious friends? Although these factors do say something about the fame and prestige of a school, the key to good reputation is whether the group you want to move among in later years considers it a high-quality institution. Your teachers will know a little about this, as will your peers. However, it is much better to consult with college and graduate students and even professionals in your field of interest, if you already know what that is.

It's safe to say that the more selective a school, the better its reputation. Good schools are swamped with applicants because their students give direct or indirect evidence of an enriching experience, graduates gain admission to good graduate and professional schools, their alumni become successful, powerful or otherwise well known. The status of a school can be evaluated further by checking out its accreditation, the size and scope of the library, the proportion of good teachers, researchers, academic scholars and writers on the faculty, and the range and relative strengths of its academic departments. After all is said and done, you should bear in mind that reputation is an elusive concept, and while you should learn what other people think about the schools you're considering, it's ultimately your own choice. Your own values should attract you to the schools that are right for you.

There are some specific ways you can check on a school's reputation. If you think you may eventually go to graduate school you should ask where last year's graduates were admitted. Did those people who wanted to go to medical school or law school get in? If you will be seeking employment after graduation you will want to know what recruiters come to the school. All colleges have offices of graduate and career planning which can furnish this sort of information.

# III
## Sweet Are the Uses of Diversity

Colleges serve varying needs. Liberal arts colleges, engineering schools, teachers colleges, military academies, schools of business administration, nursing colleges, agricultural and technical schools and art schools—all have evolved in response to the requirements of individuals or society. Most universities offer concentrations in many areas. There is an incredible diversity of specialized programs in education, agronomy, physical therapy, aeronautical engineering, speech pathology or home economics. Ask guidance counselors, write to professional associations and consult guidebooks and college catalogs to discover the opportunities in your area of interest.

Many small schools are excellent in certain specialized areas. Elementary schoolteachers graduating from Lesley College in Cambridge have better job opportunities than graduates of schools with considerably more clout in other areas. Parsons School of Design trains fine artists and a Wharton School of Finance degree is perhaps the best undergraduate business credential. Cornell's School of Hotel Administration gives self-contained specialty training within the larger university.

Are you ready to specialize at the Juilliard School or would you prefer to combine your music training with a liberal arts education at Oberlin, which has an excellent but less professionally oriented music program? The international relations department at George Washington and the marine biology department at Miami receive much greater acclaim than the rest of the university.

Students dreading another decade of formal education might consider accelerated programs like Boston University's and Northwestern's six-year medical-degree program. Brown has a novel six-year medical-science program: graduates are prepared for medical research and attend excellent medical schools for their last two years of training. Colleges like Northeastern and Antioch offer cooperative programs that coordinate education with work experience. Some colleges, Sweet Briar, for example, encourage study in foreign countries, and there is one, Chapman College in California, that even provides an around-the-world cruise for its students.

If you are not ready for a four-year plunge consider two-year junior colleges or community colleges (local, publicly funded two-year colleges, where tuition costs are low and one can economically live at home). These colleges enable students to gain specialized vocational training, obtain a two-year associate degree in arts or science, or pursue a two-year parallel program geared to transferring to a four-year school. They generally have more relaxed admission standards than traditional four-year schools. If you haven't been getting good grades but want to continue in school, you might try a junior college, where the academic pressure is relatively light, and you can get into the swing of studying effectively.

Another kind of junior college is the all-girl school that was formerly known as a "finishing school." Though the emphasis has shifted slightly at these schools, they still stress skills useful in the upper reaches of society, such as an appreciation of the arts, polished manners and "gracefulness." Today most of these schools provide an acceptable two-year education as well. Pine Manor Junior College seems to be the best of the set, which also includes Bradford, Bennett, Green Mountain, Mount Vernon, Endicott and Harcum junior colleges. In recent years, women who have come out of these schools have transferred to the best colleges and universities in the country.

Applicants who think they may be interested in transferring at a later point in their careers should investigate the success of the college's graduates in transfer placement. Some states, notably California, provide extensive opportunities to transfer from junior colleges to four-year institutions within the state university system. In addition to several basketball players of national fame, thousands of less coordinated individuals have traveled this route to UCLA and Berkeley. Some four-year universities offer a two-year program for students who are unsure of their desire or ability to make the long haul. Graduates of Boston University's two-year College of Basic Studies and Ohio State's School of General Studies have an excellent chance of moving into the four-year university.

One difference between universities and colleges is that the former award graduate degrees. Within Columbia University, for example, you might be an undergraduate at Columbia College or studying for your doctorate at the Division of Graduate Faculties. Some graduate and professional schools give preference to graduates of their college. Case Western Reserve and Washington University are both good universities with excellent medical schools that preferentially admit their own college graduates. Harvard and Yale have their own professional schools, and according to their catalogs, their undergraduates are given preference. Often, interested students who meet the requirements are allowed to take graduate courses while they are still undergraduates. They get a chance to know the professor and may get a recommendation from him when they apply to graduate schools. In these applications, recommendations carry a lot of weight, and a letter from a member of the faculty of the graduate school is impressive.

## *Life Style*

Visit the campuses of schools you will apply to, if you can. Do students seem interested and happy or uptight and intense? Are studying and socializing competitive? Do the pre-meds sneak impurities into the products of experiments in an attempt to raise their own standing, or do the students discuss their courses and share in the learning process? What's the fashion mode—work shirts or Saks Fifth Avenue? Are teachers faculty or friends? What are the social pressures and rewards? Do students get high on grass or Schlitz? The way students relate to each other, their values, and the collective personality of each campus greatly influence whether you will be happy at a particular college. It is usually impossible to read about attitudes and personalities and unwise to rely solely on the evaluation of others.

Many schools provide tours given by students who can

answer questions about the college. Do not restrict yourself to the official viewpoint. You won't be formally introduced to dissidents or malcontents, so further exploration is advisable. You will find wandering students very receptive to "I am thinking of applying here. What's it like?" You will most often receive direct answers: "It's fun, but you don't learn a thing"; "Everyone works their ass off around here"; "The campus is ready to explode." Maintain a certain perspective. It may be the style to knock the school. Students on academic probation may criticize the quality of the education, and a radical with an exaggerated sense of power may warn you of a never-to-take-place explosion. Also, a student saddled with a semester of particularly difficult or unexpectedly boring courses may be unfairly negative about the school.

A college enthusiastically described as "a real gas, wild fraternity parties, swinging chicks and a great bunch of guys" may seem anachronistic to you. Is fraternity life important, and do "in" campus groups dominate the social life? What are the parietal regulations like? Are relations between the sexes relaxed and easy or frantic and frustrated? Will heavy work loads limit your free time? Are people happy? A school everyone leaves on weekends may not be your idea of a satisfying academic and social community.

Will your impatience with existing institutions be shared by your classmates? Will your "over thirty" conservatism be tolerated? Are political differences discussed and respected or is the campus polarized by mutual distrust and dislike? You should seek an atmosphere free of intolerance and repression, open or disguised. The free exchange of ideas is an essential ingredient in your education.

Try to meet with some faculty members. Their willingness to meet with you says something about the college. Ask students about professors. Are they good? Can you get to see them? Do they socialize with students? For another perspective, ask teachers about the students. What are they like? What are their interests?

Talk with many people. Test your values against theirs. Are the students preoccupied with money and possessions? A financial struggle through a school where all your friends own and value sports cars in not much fun. Observe laughter and hand-holding, style of dress, length of hair, diversity and homogeneity and pungent smoke in the courtyard air. Go so far as to make a list of the ten things most important in your life style. Are they too hard to find?

Ask people you meet about the school's deficiencies. Get their opinions on your other choices. Many of them have considered or applied to your other selections and have friends who go there.

## Physical Environment

### Urban—Rural

Do you need the trees, grass and woods a campus could provide or would you blossom in an urban concrete university? It's rare to find a campus that successfully combines the qualities of town and country. You can opt for pleasant surroundings, space to stretch in, clean air, pretty vegetation, but you may suffer an attendant stir-craziness brought on by isolation from civilization and what comes to be known as "real life." Or, if you choose the vibrant life of the city, its many types of people, the availability of all kinds of goods and first-run movies, you may find that you've got coffee jitters even before you take your first morning cup. Unfortunately, visiting a school won't tell you much about your real reactions to its ambience, for novelty will cripple your judgment. It's a simple proposition, but one that must get hard consideration: don't break your neck getting in, don't plan on living for several years in a place you aren't going to like.

### Large–Small

What's your reaction to massive impersonality? Would you be brought down by: passing five hundred students on your way to class and not knowing anyone, watching a television instead of a teacher, sitting among fifteen hundred students in an auditorium classroom? For many, the university megalopolis is an extension of the society outside, passably efficient but monumentally cold. For others, a big school is a constantly expanding universe, alive and always surprising. It allows privacy and greater ability to cut classes without being noticed, endless new social encounters and a great variety of courses and cultural events.

It's likely that you will be impressed by a visit to a small college, for as a rule these schools are distinguished by charming architecture or an outright beautiful campus. However, bear in mind that after a few months you may be turned off by invasive familiarity: fifty students in the dining room knowing whom you are dating, one professor teaching half the courses in your major, and meeting the boy you were "too sick to see" at the only movie in town. The small campus is the analog of the small town with its imposing sense of community. If you don't dig that, keep away. For many people, on the other hand, small colleges provide an attractive warmth, a sense of belonging. Small colleges offer more faculty contact and greater access to the athletic, cultural and academic facilities. It's relatively easy, at these schools, to find recognition, the constant reinforcement of "Hi, George, how's it going," the opportunity to be a leader, a star athlete, a campus celebrity.

Don't accept all the clichés about large and small schools. Students do establish close relations with faculty members at large universities, especially as they begin to take more advanced and specialized courses. It is possible to maintain a private life on a small campus, and to live in a small dormitory at a large school that offers warmth and familiar faces. Small schools can be cold, and large schools may offer a poor selection of courses. Many schools have attempted to combine the advantages of both worlds. Harvard and Yale have residential houses with affiliated faculty so that students can experience the community and personal interaction of a small unit within the context of a multi-university. The Associated Colleges at Claremont, the University of California at Santa Cruz and the Atlanta University Center have attemped to integrate the features of large and small through a cooperative system. In this group plan several small colleges cluster around a common campus and common facilities and share facilities and cultural events while maintaining social and organizational autonomy. For each of your choices, evaluate the actual situations of class size, course offerings, faculty contact, privacy and student relations. Think in terms of individual qualities, not mere numbers.

### Shelter

Where are you going to sleep? Four postpubescent years of sharing a bedroom can pose some challenging problems. However, college may be the first time in your life you'll be able to share a room—a room that is your total living space —an exercise which can make you a better friend and mate.

At most schools, all freshmen must live in dorms, so, at best, you're only given the option of stating a preferred roommate. High school friends often think they want to live together. This has caused the breakup of many a beautiful friendship, although some people recommend it as against the "pig in a poke" method. One thing is certain: freshman roommate relationships tend to be, in one way or another, intense because of the many new situations encountered and the generally high level of energy expended. No matter whom you live with, beware of becoming too interdependent: an "It's us partners against the world" attitude is comforting, but not too broadening. If you're given a choice of living on or off campus, and don't have immediate strong feelings one way or another, live in the dorm your first year. It can provide a framework in new and sometimes confusing surroundings. It's a unique experience that most people recall with pleasure. At the worst, it can force you to do some compromising, and you can always move out.

After a year or two, the tie on the doorknob advising you that one of your roommates is occupied might become a drag. In the later years of your collegiate career, you may want more freedom and independence. Look on and off campus for comfort, space and price. Are satisfactory alternatives available? Can you afford them?

### Food

What are you going to eat? Institutional food ranges from adequate to awful. Though it isn't so important that it should be the sole basis of your decision, four years of awful food can be unpleasant or result in large expenditures at the student union or the local pizza joint. If you visit the college, try to eat a couple of meals in the dining hall, and get opinions from the regular diners, bearing in mind that responses will make meals sound a bit worse than they are. If you live in the dorms are you required to take your meals there? Can you pay separately for room and board?

### Athletics

Sports are very important to many of us in terms of competition, physical conditioning, breaking the tension of academics. Yet some students find themselves a thousand miles from a decent ski area, at schools without tennis or squash facilities, where the pool is exclusively for class or swim-team use or where the athletic facilities are clear across town.

With a few exceptions, rah-rah big-time football is played west of the Mississippi and south of the Mason-Dixon line. Do you care? Are you good enough to play varsity ball? You might make the football team at many small schools, though you would not be qualified for water boy on the last place team in the Big Ten. Are athletes campus heroes or are they viewed as anachronisms and alumni pacifiers? Do you want an opportunity to make the pros? Some schools, like Grambling College, are famous for their productivity of professional athletes. What are the opportunities for women in sports? For you amateur players, are there facilities available, intramural programs, fraternities in league competition?

## *Coeducation*

One wonders how a large segment of the academic community resisted for so long, but at last coeducation is becoming a universal phenomenon. At coed schools one need not travel fifty miles for a date. Meeting someone for coffee in the middle of the week consumes only an hour and constitutes no real threat or weekend commitment. When members of the opposite sex are plentiful you can proceed at a relaxed pace in forming friendships. The presence of both halves of the thinking world can improve and enliven the classroom experience.

Some young women at Dartmouth, Williams, Wesleyan, Colgate or other "transition schools" love the experience; others complain about the faculty's residual anti-female prejudice and about the unnatural social stress of being so few and so new among so many. However, on the whole, the opportunities are encouraging, and certainly the social atmosphere is an improvement over the old-time strained and frenzied weekend social functions. Similarly, men can find their company actively sought at Vassar, Bennington and Sarah Lawrence. You no longer need a glib opener or the confidence of Joe Namath to approach attractive women. The friendship can mature gracefully, fostered by proximity and shared experiences.

Ironically, many who had eagerly looked forward to life

at newly liberated schools find themselves peculiarly isolated. Men, socialized to expect weakness and emotionalism from women, find it difficult to respect their opinions. Women, socialized to expect insensitivity and sexual aggression from men, don't easily reveal themselves in conversation. One student described a newly integrated college as "a women's school working out a classic male chauvinist syndrome."

Adjustment at any coed school goes beyond learning to wash your hair in converted urinals or eating cottage cheese for lunch. It is difficult to maintain a real sense of privacy when you can be in a "social situation" at 8:00 A.M. over a plate of scrambled eggs. Everyone knows whom you were with last night and this exposure can have a disastrous effect on your social mystique. It may be a struggle to build meaningful friendships. As one Yale graduate remarked with painful wonder, "I never expected to leave here single and I certainly never expected to graduate a virgin, but somehow I managed to do both."

The antithesis of the transition school is the exclusively men's or women's college. Male colleges have practically disappeared, but women have a unique opportunity to attend Wellesley, Smith, Skidmore, Beaver or other all-women schools, which three years ago may not have finished reading their applications. In a recent year Mount Holyoke accepted 60 percent of all applicants, so numerous are those who elect to go to newly coed schools.

You can enjoy the pleasures of coeducation while attending certain all-male or all-female institutions. Coordinate colleges like Harvard/Radcliffe, Hamilton/Kirkland and

Tulane/Sophie Newcomb are coed in every respect but name.

## The Institutional Personality

### A Free Thinker

Some schools are traditional and rigid, prescribing specific courses and programs. MIT, for example, demands virtually the same academic program of all freshmen. Certain colleges may require English composition courses, two years of a foreign language or a particular distribution of courses in different fields. Find out if a school dictates courses, insists on a fixed number of exams and papers, and imposes an inflexible set of requirements upon students. Catalogs are explicit about educational policies. Professors and students at the school can place the catalog in perspective and tell you whether exceptions are made.

If science isn't your forte, imagine the ordeal of a physics course "for your own good." A useless language requirement has delayed the graduation of many students. On the other hand, if you are uncertain about your interests a prescribed curriculum may provide the best introduction to a variety of fields. The school may give you enough freedom so that their prescription is not unpalatable. The point is to know what the school requires before making your application.

A number of colleges offer progressive educational alternatives. Hampshire in Massachusetts, New College in Florida, Antioch in Ohio, Goddard in Vermont and Colorado College are examples of institutions offering high-quality education and a maximum of personal freedom. Course requirements are virtually nonexistent. Faculty members may be friends and receptive to new ideas for courses or projects. Work is not neatly apportioned into four-credit units. A student may spend ten units or an entire semester on an analysis of the juvenile court system. Grades don't exist and exams are an educational tool. The appeal of the progressive colleges has contributed to the recent decline in applications to the traditional Ivy League schools. This development will mean more openings at some prestige colleges and greater pressure on these colleges to change over the next few years.

Do you want a school that has abandoned grades or restricts evaluation to pass–fail? People on campus will be able to tell you if the pass–fail system makes for a relaxed, low-pressure environment or for competition that may be more subtle but just as intense as the old fight for A's and B's. Some schools use "pass with honors," "high pass," "pass," and "fail," which seem almost to duplicate the traditional system. For your particular field, will graduate school admissions and immediate employment be difficult if all you can present is a series of P's?

### Grading System

High school lunchroom conversations abound with "Is he [or she] a good grader?" Should you ask the same question about Harvard, Swarthmore and the University of Chicago? Unequivocally yes! All three institutions admit a select student body, but Swarthmore and Chicago give lower grades than Harvard for the same-quality work. They believe median performance should be evaluated as C, while Harvard likes to think of its median as a B student and it graduates over 70 percent of a typical class with honors. With the same amount of work it's easier to get good grades at Harvard. Many schools view the freshman year as an obstacle course and automatically eliminate a fixed percentage of the class. Other colleges try to go easy on freshmen. Your success in college could depend on the way your college evaluates its students.

Some graduate schools place great weight on the ABC's of grading in evaluating candidates for admission. And while Swarthmore graduates are of the highest caliber, many of them believe their chances for graduate appointments are reduced because of the rigid grading system. It is easy to learn whether or not a school gives good grades. Some schools post grades at the end of the term. Any professor or student can tell you how the median performance is evaluated. As an applicant, you must ask yourself if grades will play a role in your plans. Will you lose out on a good graduate school? Graduate schools aside, will you be embarrassed with a B— average even if you are in the top quarter of your class? You can determine the prejudicial effect of a low grading system by checking graduate admissions from a particular college. Start by inquiring at the career-planning office.

### Responsiveness to Change

Has the administration been "with it"? In recent years the underpinnings of many of our universities and the basic assumptions of their existence have been shaken by issues such as ROTC, minority admissions, black studies, community and labor relations, faculty employment, grades, student participation in running the university, academic freedom, government research and the limits of dissent. Change is likely to continue and many universities may again be paralyzed by a confusion of administrative recalcitrance and student provocation.

You might get your kicks by shutting down a minor megalopolis or you may prefer an uninterrupted four-year education at an institution responsive to reasonable student demands. Radical political activity with far-reaching consequences seems to thrive at Berkeley and Wisconsin. Many schools have so kept up with the times that focal points of organized discontent are hard to come by. Decide whether you prefer four years of confrontation and turmoil or a more peaceful college experience.

### Religion

At Notre Dame, Bob Jones, Yeshiva and Brigham Young, to name a few among the many schools founded on religious principles, you are never completely free of the prevailing religious thought on campus. For some students this presents a unique opportunity to combine a university education with the study of theology and a religious atmosphere. For others, it's just a drag. Consider how much formal and informal attention to religion is required, how much you want, how much you can avoid. To what extent does a parochial bent interfere with the unfettered pursuit of knowledge and self-development? If houses of worship make you uncomfortable, God is just a childhood memory, and the Bible is not your idea of good reading, do not go to a church-related school. A little thing like required convocation once a month can become annoying out of all proportion to the time it takes.

Many schools with religious roots, like Harvard, Brown, Colgate and Columbia, have become completely non-sectarian, while other schools have maintained their original ties. Check this out before you apply.

## Individual Factors

Although it may be important to be with old friends, to go to Dad's alma mater or to be near big brother and have use of his car, do not be unduly bound by family traditions or influenced by the urgings of friends. Evaluate the reasons others give for going to a particular school against your own values, interests and goals. Friends who suggest you should stick together may be insecure about the uncertainty of a new experience. It is easy to make new friends. Don't be foolishly bound to old ties which could stifle this unique opportunity for personal growth.

A college may offer you a special program, a large scholarship, freedom from basic requirements, the opportunity to work with a particular professor, study in foreign countries, an evening program, or a degree after only three years. Kosher food, a Greek Orthodox Church or a nearby Spanish-speaking community may be important to you.

Finally, your high school may share a special relationship with certain schools. Andover obviously sends lots of its graduates to Harvard. St. Paul's in Minnesota and Trinity in New York do well at Princeton. Certain public high schools have a good record at state universities. Your guidance counselor is particularly aware of colleges which have had good experiences with your high school's graduates. He can also prevent you from sending an application to a college which invariably rejects applicants from your school.

In making your selection, look inward and determine who and where you are at this stage of your life. Even if you are uncertain, part of life is realizing that we all continually make important decisions amidst confusion. One difference between a crazy mixed-up adolescent and his crazy mixed-up parents is the ability of the latter simply to *make* decisions in spite of confusion. So, after evaluating all the evidence, you must decide how you, and not your two closest friends, want to spend your next four years. And keep cool. If you're wrong you can always transfer.

## Recent Trends—What's Happenin', Baby

A dean of admissions at a large private New England university was asked to describe an applicant guaranteed admission to his school. He replied, "Rich, beautiful, brilliant, talented or just plain black." Things are happening every year which significantly change previous admission patterns.

### The Times They Are A-Changin'

If you are black, Puerto Rican, Indian or Mexican, you are in great demand. In a belated twinge of conscience American Academia has decided to carry the white man's burden to your front door. Even if your high school training was inadequate, many good schools will accept you and offer special training during summer sessions and throughout your academic career.

Guidance counselors at small schools often are not aware of the many changing opportunities offered by schools across the country. Harvard, Dartmouth, Amherst and dozens of similar institutions are vigorously seeking to diversify their student bodies. Write to the schools you are interested in, and mention your background. Admission is still competitive but you'll move onto a quicker line.

Unfortunately, the acceptance of minority students does eliminate a certain group of not-so-qualified white students who formerly made top schools as part of a high-risk pool. There were those students, classified as underachievers with great potential, who, while not qualified in terms of traditional criteria, showed sufficient promise to justify the risk of accepting them.

### Ground Breaking and Student Making

Disenchantment with degree programs in science and engineering has been the natural reaction to recent space-program and private-industry cutbacks. The fate of Cape Kennedy and Seattle demonstrate the expendability of university-trained technicians. The expanding and contracting demand for certain specialists will have the result of periodically discouraging college students from entering these areas of study.

Universities have been spending millions of dollars on science facilities and faculties. New buildings must be filled, expensive professors need students, and the smaller number of applicants interested in science must be given every break. One Ivy League school has indicated they are currently accepting science students who previously would have been discards.

Planning, budgeting, programming and building occur long before adversity is felt. Look for new construction. When a school has built a new math building, cyclotron, psychology lab, music building, or drama center, you can be assured that they will be searching for students to use the facilities.

If you're quite undecided about a major field of study, apply in one that needs people. Even if you know your interest but are afraid you won't make the grade for, say, the old and established school of arts and sciences, apply in one of the divisions that want students, and transfer later to the department of your choice.

### Do-It-Yourself Prognosis

Analyzing recent acceptance trends is vital to selecting a college. Every week new information enters the picture, such as the admitting of the opposite sex to one-time all-women or all-men schools and, more recently, open admissions, which has made college acceptance a reality for any high school graduate in New York City. Johns Hopkins now admits exceptional high school students after their junior year. In the next few years colleges will be initiating "external"-degree programs, where attendance on campus will not be required. At many colleges a bachelor's degree will be granted after three years of study. And at still others, students may be encouraged to defer attendance for a year to experience another style of life. Minority admissions, economic recession, new construction and disenchantment with certain fields are examples of recent trends having great impact on college admissions.

## *Waitlessness—Early Decision*

If you can narrow your choice down to one school, there is a way of shortening the lengthy limbo period in which you sweat out the school's decision. It is called "early decision" and is offered by schools as diverse as Kenyon College, Bryn Mawr, Michigan, Cedar Crest, Goucher, Vassar, Hollins, Mount Holyoke, Amherst, Randolph-Macon, Wilson, Skidmore, Hood, Salem, Connecticut and hundreds more. Harvard, Yale and many other colleges do not have early admission and you should check the availability of the plan at all your choices before applying.

The early-decision plan is designed for the student who knows his mind and whose record leaves little question in the college's view. Many good schools accept so many students on an early-decision basis that a regular application is almost futile. Not filing for early decision indicates to many colleges that they are not your first choice.

Early decision requires advance planning, but it can mean an acceptance before New Year's Day. Most early-decision applications demand a pledge to enroll if admitted, although schools like MIT and Georgetown offer the security of an early acceptance along with the freedom to apply elsewhere. You should note carefully the particulars of this plan at each school you consider.

If you are not accepted in the early-decision process, you will either be rejected or deferred and considered again with the entire applicant pool in the spring.

A student interested in early decision should be aware that

1. The deadline for applications is generally in October;
2. You must present the required College Board scores, which means you should take the SAT's and Achievements in March, May or July of your junior year;
3. You must, with a few exceptions, sign a statement assuring the college that you will attend if admitted.

If you say you will enroll if accepted, you had better mean it. Going back on your word speaks badly of your own maturity and sense of responsibility, angers the college and embarrasses your high school. Since any subsequent application must be made with the high school's cooperation, do not expect enthusiasm if you renege on your commitment.

## Geographical Quotas

### Preference or Prejudice

Many schools have carefully considered the question of geographic distribution and have evolved firm policies, largely in an attempt to achieve a balanced and diversified student body. Students with 600 boards and B averages can be rejected from selective schools in their part of the country despite their capabilities. If, for example, you are from New York, which annually sends forth tens of thousands of students, you may resent geographical quotas by which Ivy League schools reject you and accept someone with lower qualifications from the Far West or the South. You increase your chances for admission by choosing schools in other areas, schools to which other top candidates in your area do not apply. Transcend your provincialism and apply to Reed in Oregon, Occidental in California, Grinnell in Iowa, Rice in Texas, Carleton in Minnesota or Kenyon in Ohio. Each is an excellent institution which should find you at least geographically desirable. Westerners who are attracted to Stanford might find Dartmouth, Amherst or Smith more receptive. The experience of living in another part of the country is likely to prove valuable as well.

Some students from New York feel that they have recently been rejected from California state schools because of an effort to thwart migration of potential political activists, many of whom are assumed to come from New York. Whatever the case, the California Board of Regents may be reacting in the only way they can to a massive increase in applications from their own state.

A few universities accept the best-qualified applicants regardless of where they are from and let the geographic distribution chart its own course. A quick perusal of a catalog will reveal whether your region is in excess or in demand at a particular institution.

## *How Do You Get Started?*

College guides and manuals can help you in your initial efforts to form a list of possible schools. Take a look first at the *Comparative Guide to American Colleges,* by James Cass and Max Birnbaum, published by Harper and Row. This book analyzes every accredited four-year college in the United States. For a more subjective approach, see *Insider's Guide to Colleges,* compiled by the staff of the *Yale Daily News,* and published by Berkeley. Other popular books are *Einstein's College Entrance Guide,* published by Grosset and Dunlap; *Lovejoy's College Guide,* published by Simon and Schuster; and *Barron's Profile of American Colleges.* If you need help narrowing the field of the hundreds of colleges across the country, you might try *The New York Times Guide to College Selection,* by Ella Mazel, published by Quadrangle Books. It intends to act as a "computer," matching your needs to what the schools can offer. Bookstores are likely to have at least one of these manuals, especially in the late summer and fall, and libraries will probably have more.

## *Safety and Numbers*

"Do I have a chance?" "Will I get in anywhere?" "How many applications can I make?"

There are no firm answers to these questions. You should apply to colleges you wish to attend if you have a reasonable chance of acceptance. Do not rely exclusively on the advice of your guidance counselor in selecting these schools. The counselor is an adviser, not an oracle. Students are often discouraged by such mentors from applying to colleges that might accept them; and sometimes the counselor's misplaced optimism results in attendance at a last-minute desperation choice. Too often a guidance counselor is unaware of all the recent trends and new policies of universities and of the special qualities the student possesses. College selection should be made with reference to many sources—parents, classmates, college students, books, college catalogs, as well as your guidance counselor.

If your house burns down, that is a disaster. If you do not have insurance, that is a complete disaster. An "insurance" or "safe" school is one where there is little chance of rejection. It is a cushion to soften the blow of rejection from your other choices.

The college where your uncle is president, a state university with a predictable admissions policy, a school which consistently accepts applicants with unspectacular qualifications, a school that advises you of your acceptance at a preliminary interview, or a school that accepts everyone—all are relatively safe schools. Assess your qualifications realistically and select enough safe schools to avoid apoplexy.

Don't, in an effort to be safe, sacrifice the impossible dream and risk a real sense of loss, a frustrated yearning for the schools you might have made. Apply to your dream schools *and* make sure there's one college on your list that's truly safe.

There can be external limitations on the number of applications you can make. Colleges often require a fifteen- or twenty-dollar application fee. Even if you can afford an unlimited number of applications, a more sinister restriction is imposed by many high schools where inadequate clerical help limits the number of applications each student can make. Five applications seem barely sufficient to permit the full expression of your hopes and desires, but when the number goes as low as three or four it's time to do something. Organize, protest, demand more applications, picket, have your parents scream, and most important, volunteer to help with the clerical work. Schools don't pose arbitrary restrictions; they are often in desperate need of more staff. They should welcome your assistance. Three shots at a target as crucial as college are appallingly few.

# IV

# The Greening of the Application

*How Admissions Committees Work*

Each year a typical admissions committee must judge thousands of applicants. How are decisions made? Understanding the workings of these committees increases your chances of a "yes."

No application is considered until all forms, fees, recommendations, transcripts and test scores have been received. In most cases, two individuals read an application, make written comments of one or two paragraphs and assign a score. The first reader is usually an admissions officer who travels to high schools in a certain region, such as the Deep South. He is accordingly designated the staff specialist on Deep Southerners. The second reader may also be an admissions officer or sometimes a faculty member. These officials develop instincts to evaluate quickly. It is because of their limited time that you must make your application readable, explain blanks and describe activities clearly and impressively.

Most colleges use a rating system—verbal, numerical or hieroglyphic. For example, on a scale of ten, five is average, one a reject, and everyone loves a ten. Significant disparity in the two scores may lead to a third reading.

Decisions are reached in committee. The chairmanship

rotates among the regional staff members. In this way the individual high school becomes an important context for the decision. Academic standards, the nature of extra-curricular activities and the performance of prior graduates are assessed. Since classmates are thus presented together, discrepancies, odd forms of the truth and outright lies are likely to be detected. Someone is bound to be the loser when two senior class presidents materialize from one school.

The chairman states the name of the applicant, his school, and the readers' scores. Ratings of 1 or 2, or their equivalents, result in swift rejection. A score of 9 or 10 brings acceptance and self-congratulations, along with slight concern about competing schools. Applicants in the middle range receive closer scrutiny. Excerpts from applications are passed around the table. To avoid the stigma of depersonalization, the admissions committee focuses on the essays, recommendations and interview. These are often read aloud as the committee struggles to evaluate the paper applicant. Inconsistencies are noted. Sincerity, sensitivity, creativity, thoughtfulness are evaluated.

In the seemingly endless flow of applications, the workings of the committee can become one of drab routine. Passionate advocacy (or objection) by one member can move the weary group to acceptance (or rejection). Applicants are accepted, rejected or put on a waiting list. Candidates who are placed on the waiting list are considered second-string players who make the first team only after some regulars go elsewhere. A student on the waiting list has a fair chance of admission, but should send a deposit to his best acceptance while awaiting the outcome.

## The Form

Applying to college can be a tedious, dehumanizing and traumatic experience and at the same time a creative process, effective and satisfying. Like clay in the hands of a sculptor, your application can be molded into an attractive self-portrait which will be judged favorably by the admissions committee.

It is not easy to create an impressive image. Colleges demand neatness, good spelling and compliance with deadlines. The race is not to the swift, but to the agile.

The first hurdle is obtaining the application. Don't write:

> Dear Sir:
> Please send me an application.

Such a request is likely to produce the following response:

> Dear Sir:
> With reference to your request for an application and/or catalog you have failed to furnish the date of your proposed entry and the division of the university to which you will apply. As soon as we receive this information we will forward all necessary materials.
> > Sincerely,
> > Admissions Committee
> > University of Pleasant Valley

A postcard or note like the following will save time and postage.

Gentlemen:

I am entering my senior year at Central Bloomsburg High School in Mayfield, Indiana, and am interested in applying for admission to Ball State College for the fall of 197–. I hope to pursue a program in business administration. Please send me an application blank, scholarship forms, catalog and any other admissions information.

Sincerely,<br>
[Name]<br>
[Address]

Don't spend time formulating application requests that are more specific or more gracefully composed. These letters are usually answered by a secretary and then discarded. The inquiry should be made early: for most colleges this means the summer following your junior year.

The formal application asks for biographical data, activities and interests, and one or more thoughtful essays. Your school will send your transcript when you make an official request, and the College Board people, when asked, will forward your test scores. Other components of the application process (discussed in following chapters) are recommendations and the personal interview; the latter is not required by all schools.

Develop a system for directing the massive flow of forms, requests, letters and transcripts. It is very helpful to make a chart with the required steps down the left margin and the schools across the top. Record the dates you take each step and check periodically to avoid tie-ups.

| | Princeton | Ursinus | Citadel | Memphis State |
|---|---|---|---|---|
| APPLICATION REQUESTED | | | | |
| APPLICATION RECEIVED | | | | |
| APPLICATION FILED | | | | |
| APPLICATION FEE SENT | | | | |
| HIGH SCHOOL GIVEN FORMS | | | | |
| HIGH SCHOOL FORMS SENT | | | | |
| MR. SMITH GIVEN REC. FORM | | | | |
| SMITH'S RECOMMENDATION SENT | | | | |
| MISS JONES GIVEN REC. FORM | | | | |
| JONES'S RECOMMENDATION SENT | | | | |
| MRS. BROWN GIVEN REC. FORM | | | | |
| BROWN'S RECOMMENDATION SENT | | | | |
| COLLEGE BOARDS REQUESTED TO BE SENT | | | | |
| INTERVIEW APPOINTMENT | | | | |
| SCHOLARSHIP APPLICATION SENT | | | | |

## *What Do You Say to a Naked Application?*

All schools require certain basic information. The sections from applications presented in this chapter are composites of many. Use them as work sheets, either writing in the book or listing separately all possible answers or entries. For example, under "Work experience" note every job you have ever held, whether or not you were paid. Refer to this comprehensive list when you fill out actual applications, selecting specific items and tailoring them to particular forms.

Study a school's application and then, on a separate sheet, compose a draft that satisfies you. Put it aside for a week. Then review it, judging the impression it will make on an admissions committee, and if necessary, make revisions before neatly completing the form and sending it off.

### Background: The Facts of Life

The opening section of a typical application is relatively straightforward. It focuses on questions like your name, address, birth date and social security number. That's right—social security number! To apply to most colleges you must first formally enroll in the United States work force.

Here's a sample biographical data section.

(Type or print)

Name in full  _____
                    (last)           (first)          (middle)

Permanent home address  _____
                              (street address)        (apartment)

                        _____
                        (city)   (state)   (zip)   (phone)

Date of birth _____ Citizenship _____ Social Security No. _____

Height _____ Weight _____ General Health _____

If you have an unusual medical history
or disability, please explain  _____

Father's full name  _____ Is he living? _____

His home address _____

His occupation _____ His educational background _____

Mother's full name _____ Is she living? _____

Her home address _____

Her occupation _____ Her educational background _____

Are parents divorced? _____ Separated? _____ If you have a legal guardian, give name and address _____

Name and address of someone besides parent or guardian who can be contacted in case of emergency _____

Brothers: number ____ ages____ Sisters: number ____ ages ____

Brothers' colleges _____ Sisters' colleges _____

List in chronological order all the schools you have attended in the last five years

| Name of school | Location | Dates attended |
|---|---|---|
|  |  |  |
|  |  |  |

Rank in
graduating class _____Class size _____

Composite academic
average for four years _____

If, during the regular term, you left
school for more than three months,
state how you were occupied _____

Work Experience: include part-time and full-time summer jobs

| Employer | Type of work you did | Dates |
|---|---|---|
|  |  |  |
|  |  |  |
|  |  |  |

Have you traveled?

Have you previously applied for admission?_____ If so, when?_____

Dates of Scholastic Aptitude Tests: Have taken ____ Will take____

Which Achievement Tests are you submitting? _____

Recommendations:    Name          Address         Position

_____

_____

_____

Relationship, name, and class of relatives who are alumni or present
students _____

_____

Where else have you applied? _____

Seemingly innocuous questions can have far-reaching
consequences. The most insidious example is "Where else
have you applied?" Schools want to be wanted and they
may reject applicants who have serious intentions elsewhere,
particularly when good colleges feel they are your fourth
choice. By offering you a place they risk losing another student who is more likely to show up in September. Avoid
admitting that you've applied to schools of disparate quality.
One way to avoid signaling clear preferences is to apply to
schools in ascending order of reputation. For example, apply
to Syracuse first, and if asked, state that you have applied
nowhere else. The next application to New York University
can list Syracuse. Cornell can be told you have applied to
Syracuse and NYU, and you can list all your other choices
on your Harvard application. If you've already applied to
several colleges, you can selectively list two or three on each
application. You might even indicate you are undecided
about other schools, although colleges will be suspicious of
a student who has no second choices.

Years ago people listed father's occupation as "sanitation

engineer" when he was a garbageman, and as "jeweler" when he was a pawnbroker. Today, it is fashionable to be a pawnbroker, an Indian steelworker or the owner of a Chinese laundry. Ethnics and novelties are in. Fancy titles are out. Children of garbagemen, truckdrivers and laborers get larger scholarships. Your application can be consistent with your scholarship form. If a school doesn't want you because your father works hard, forget it.

## Activities and Interests—You Are What You Do

The successful applicant conveys a consistent and a consistently attractive image. There is no way to glorify your birth date or social security number, but image building can begin with your presentation of activities and interests. The way you spend your time, the books you read, and the subjects you enjoy are explored in the following sample questions:

List five extracurricular activities in order of importance to you.

Name your favorite subjects in school underlining those with which you would like to become more familiar.

How did you spend the past three summers?

Work experience—Mention responsibilities, dates, and amounts earned.

What are your educational and vocational aspirations?

Have you ever attained particular distinction, received honors or awards?

In what ways do you participate in the affairs of the community?

Questions like these don't call for essays, but are generally intended to provide short answers that are informative or descriptive. Stay as close as possible to the length indicated for the answer. The response to these questions can describe your many dimensions: joiner and/or loner, scientist and/or humanist, athlete and/or scholar, pragmatist and/or idealist.

Of course, brief entries on an application cannot be a thorough or absolute representation of a human personality and achievements, but they can, if presented skillfully, enhance your image. At the same time, the end product should not be artificially fabricated, for an unrealistic self-portrait may not hold up in the light of your high school's report and teachers' recommendations. You must think through who you are, what you've done, what you can offer, and how best to present this "you" on paper.

A young man who represents himself as a chess champion and an A student might emerge on paper as a profound but rather boring intellectual. If he mentions skill at basketball and youth-group leadership, he appears more well-rounded. However, if the same individual adds his four-line part in the school play, three club memberships, and two hall monitor positions, he reduces his self-description to meaningless braggadocio. Do not list many routine activities which can obscure real interests and blur what otherwise can be a sharp, strong impression.

Highlight hobbies and interests which distinguish you from other applicants. A rock collection, a year in Yugoslavia or a demonstrable interest in electronics indicate germinal affinities and talents. Future geologists, linguists and engineers are viewed as low-risk candidates when they've already developed their interest. The young woman with a B average and an afternoon secretarial job can be passed by as unexceptional. When she mentions, however, that her job is at a school for retarded children and involves dealing with visiting parents, this may be taken as an indication of her interest in casework as a possible career.

A demanding job can explain a D in chemistry; football season can explain a spring term consistently better than the fall term; or a sick parent can justify a weak junior year. Recent success is more significant than early failure. Colleges are often willing to accept someone who began unimpressively and is now discovering and proving himself.

The words used to describe activities, interests and honors powerfully influence the impact of the facts. Be honest but clever in giving titles to what you do. For instance, your teacher asked you to survey the class to determine the extent of dope smoking. You asked Arnold to help you and thus became the chairman of the "Drug Usage Study Committee." For a non-athlete who occasionally plays intramural badminton, "Intramural Sports" is a fair and useful credit. If you raise money for senior scholarships you could say "Fund Raising for Senior Scholarships" or "Scholarship Drive Committee." The use of "Drive" animates your description. Washing test tubes two afternoons a week for the mess you made in chem lab could qualify you as a "lab assistant." Be sure, however, that in the event a college decides to investigate, descriptions of activities are recognizable to your high school and reasonably consistent with any letters of recommendation.

Be concise in listing activities and honors. The Mayfair Food Stores John F. Kennedy Memorial Citizenship Award for Part-Time Employees would be more impressive as The John F. Kennedy Citizenship Award.

Remember, colleges value what they recognize. Familiarity with the National Honor Society makes it a more useful entry than Central High Atheneum, and Debate Club is more informative than Society of Demosthenes. The nature of school publications should be clarified. The *Springfield Echo* is unrecognizable unless it's described as a literary magazine.

Your self-portrait should be drawn within boundaries of the truth that are generous but not foolish. It is not advisable to omit "vice" from president, "co" from captain or "assistant" from editor. There is a difference between characterization and lying, and the former provides plenty of room for artfulness.

### Negative Image

Some images inevitably spell disaster. Don't waste time portraying yourself as a smart-ass or an anarchist. In fact, if you happen to be a smart-ass or an anarchist, you'll be wise also to put forward a few qualities that seem more favorable to admissions committees. Answering a serious question about your educational plans with a quip like "I plan to go to college next fall," is both foolish and unnecessary. Stating that you "synthesized tabs of organic compounds" may be clever, but it spoils the "plus" activity of being a "chemistry lab assistant."

List only items of substance. Admissions committees are not interested in the "Best Dressed Male in the Class."

A candid description of your activities as editor of the underground newspaper *Off the Pedant* may discourage the college from accepting another malcontent. Achievements like leading a student strike or being busted need not be mentioned, though if these actions are on your high school record, you should be prepared to discuss them competently and intelligently at your interviews. Those who feel compelled to expound at any opportunity and at inordinate length on repression, racism and capitalist exploitation may appear too great a risk to an admissions committee. Revolutionary ambitions and iconoclastic tendencies should either be tempered or carefully worded with attention to the probable attitudes and certain power of the admissions committee.

Colleges are sensitive to psychological instability which portends a troubled college career. Avoid comments about your domineering mother, extremely attractive father, demons and devils, or difficulty in getting others to listen to you. If you've been in therapy and it's not on your record, don't bring it up. If the college is bound to find out, initiate a discussion of the problem and explain how well you function now that it's cleared up.

### Focusing the Image

In the "Interests and Activities" part of the application, an item for which you have no answer should not be a source of anxiety, since the application is designed to allow a large number of students with varied high school careers to express themselves. You may have avoided clubs and publications because of a job, community projects, or because activities within your school seemed less important than your private development. However, you must provide the college with a basis for evaluating you. Do not leave too many glaring blank spaces. If the application asks for extracurricular activities you should type right across the available space that you worked every afternoon to support your widowed mother. That should readily excuse your nonparticipation in intramural bowling. If you are a pianist who practices five hours a day, a scientist interested in research, a voracious reader, or an independent thinker who is not an organization man, the college is likely to evaluate you on your terms. You should realize, however, that a complete absence of interests on the application may be a serious handicap in the admissions game.

Here's a summary of guidelines for the short-answer section of the application:

1. Be consistent. Coordinate your activities and interests with the rest of the material you submit to the admissions committee.

2. Read the questions carefully and answer them accurately. If the application requests five activities, list five, not more. If you have participated in only three activities, do not invent two more.

3. When limits are not stated, limit yourself to important activities. Long lists make the significant seem less so.

4. Unless otherwise directed, list activities in order of importance. Give preference to those in which you were a leader, achieved distinction, or plan to continue in college.

5. Be consistent in style. If you list one entry by activity, position and dates of participation, list all entries in that sequence.

6. Entries should be neat, legible and easily understood. If an activity like "Sing Commissioner" is not self-explanatory, indicate that you directed the junior-class musical in the annual "Sing" competition.

7. Keep copies of all application forms. Your brief statements can be the basis of long discussions at interviews, and, needless to say, forgetting your achievements may belie their truth.

## *Thought-Provoking Questions— Where the One-Liner Is Inappropriate*

*We seek those students who have curiosity about the world around them, the ability and energy to investigate that world meaningfully, and the courage to evaluate and act upon their findings. Intellectual curiosity and ability, energy and strength of character—these are qualities sought in every student admitted to Princeton.*

[Information given to candidates for admission]

In their zeal to identify the applicant superstar, colleges employ two types of essays—autobiographical and everything else. The autobiography is a special art discussed in the next chapter. Examples of "everything else" topics follow:

Ideally, what position and life style would you hope to have twenty years from now?

Name one book that has significantly influenced your thinking. Explain.

What achievement of yours pleases you most?

You are the world's greatest philosopher and about to die. What is your last message to the world?

What in your opinion is the most urgent problem facing mankind and how do you hope to contribute to its solution?

If you could have a conversation with any living person, whom would you choose?

If you never had to earn a living, what would you do with your time?

What will the world be like in 2084?

In many ways these queries are a pain in the neck. Some schools ask you to write more than one essay, so that finishing several applications can involve as much work as a semester of English. Nonetheless, it's a job that must be done well, and it is possible to simplify it. If you survey all the applications you will fill out, you'll see a lot of repetition. Prepare prototype essays on several topics and adapt them later. Refer to old essays in writing new ones. It's unnecessary to write a completely new essay for each application.

Essays effectively eliminate lazy or unenthusiastic applicants. They ease the administration's conscience about the impersonality of the system, identify a number of illiterates and psychotics, and allow the admissions staff to shape the type of student body they want. While one may question the value of these essays, the colleges do take them seriously. Some, like Sarah Lawrence, rely almost exclusively on a battery of essay questions.

Questions that are intended to inspire thought allow you to add depth to the outline of yourself. Creative approaches are encouraged. An artistic individual asked for a sketch of himself might send the committee a charcoal picture rather than a thousand words. You are not obligated to answer "Is there anything else you would like to say" questions, but if you believe you have an important thought or additional helpful information about yourself, give it.

Where a limited space is provided for an answer the school is not looking for a magnum opus. Demonstrate a competent use of the English language. Ask your English teacher to assign a few application essays rather than normal writing assignments, or ask to speak to him after class about your pilot essay. His comments can help you remove the rough edges and may stimulate some creative thought.

Instructions are to be followed. Colleges would not ask a question if they didn't want an answer. They would not specify "three activities" if they wanted more. When space is provided for your answer, do not attach extra sheets. Applications are read under pressure, and extra sheets with longer essays may make some admissions committees unhappy.

# V
## The
## Personal
## Essay

The long essay that some colleges include on applications may be called an autobiographical essay, a personal statement, a personal assessment, a philosophy of your life, or any number of terms, ranging from specific to ambiguous. In general, the intention is to encourage you to expand your self-presentation beyond the other briefer parts of the application. Some schools may want you to give a summary of your life, one which repeats the basic details but is written in an essay reflecting your personality and approach. Others will ask you to focus on a particular aspect of your life, with questions like: "How do you expect college to contribute to your personal and intellectual development?" or "Describe an experience that profoundly affected your life" or "What do you consider to be your greatest accomplishment?" A large number of colleges intentionally leave the instructions for the essay open-ended, the better to note your qualities of judgment, cleverness and resourcefulness. It's very important to read instructions carefully and understand the type of essay that is wanted.

Some schools make the long essay an optional section of the application, and students understandably shy away from this seemingly frightening task. A moment's reflection, however, will bring home the obvious benefits of taking the option. You automatically seem, if not more resourceful, certainly more energetic. You remain longer in the eye of the reader and hopefully the committee. And you have the chance to enhance, balance or simply elaborate on the other parts of your application, and to include good things about yourself that weren't asked for when you were filling in the blanks. The long essay can add a positive dimension to your application.

### Focus on a Unique Aspect of Yourself

You may see yourself as Plain Jane or Innocuous Irving, unique only because of your totally undistinguished background. Such a private evaluation is probably wrong. Most people who have lived seventeen years have done something to separate themselves from the herd. Admissions committees want to know about this. Below is a list that may help you recall details buried by application anxieties.

*Sports*
*Academic achievement*
*Overcoming physical, economic, social or other handicaps*
*Job experience, money-making schemes*
*Travel*
*Languages*
*Things you've built; gardening, model making*
*Awards*
*Unusual hobbies*
*Helping friends resolve serious problems*
*Writing poems, letters to editors, stories*
*Political campaigns*

*Heroic achievements*
*Playing musical instruments, dancing*
*Camp experiences, scouting*
*Painting, sculpting, crafts, photography*
*Religious training*
*Cheerleading*
*Community service—drug-rehabilitation groups, prison*
   *visits, reading to the blind*
*Scientific research*

The spotlighted activity or achievement or skill should demonstrate something about you—something definite, something positive, but not necessarily miraculous.

> *In junior high school I became fascinated with the microscope. At Thomas Jefferson High there was no microbiology club and during club period I initially attended the long-established biology club. It is difficult to introduce anything new to a high school fifty years old, but after much effort I managed to form a microbiology club . . .*

Although this paragraph is plain and only reasonably well written, it is a sincere and straightforward attempt by a quiet student to highlight one thing he did which distinguished him among a large student body—and it worked.

Be sure that what you believe to be unique is truly unique. In some high schools 70 percent of the girls are boosters, 80 percent of the students participate in intramurals, and 100 percent belong to some form of club—a compulsory Wednesday-afternoon eighth-period activity. When your participation in a large group activity has been extraordinary, be sure to make that clear.

## Be Positive

Many applicants use the essay space to justify all their failings. Do not say:

"I received a D in Chemistry because . . ."

"The reason I never played on any varsity team is . . ."

"The discrepancy between my boards and grades is caused by . . ."

If there is a discrepancy you must have done well on something. Why? Have you read three hundred novels in your four years of high school rather than study for exams? Emphasize your voracious reading appetite. Did you work after school rather than study? Describe an interesting aspect of your job. Did you visit museums, translate *The Iliad,* coach a Little League team? Emphasize the positive.

If there is a glaring and possibly fatal deficiency in your record, explain it in a positive way.

> *My enjoyment of literature has stirred my interest in writing. I have been composing poetry for several years but I feel I am most talented in writing short stories. Three of my stories have been published in student magazines. I plan to pursue writing as a career and know that Wellesley's English department could help me develop as a creative and proficient writer. Unfortunately, I do not exhibit much ability in math. I have failed every math course I have ever taken at least once. How-*

*ever, I did work as a cashier at a local supermarket for ten weeks without making a mistake. If math and science grades were excluded, my average would rank me as one of the top five in my class. I have straight A's in English. I am a good writer and would love to study at Wellesley to improve my skills.*

This composition projects a convincing feeling that the applicant is strongly interested in a field she intends to pursue —which is an important plus. If the school has an inflexible rule about mathematics grades, she probably will be rejected. But if her general average was 88, and Wellesley sometimes makes exceptions to a hypothetical standard of accepting no one with an average less than 90, the essay might make a difference.

If your essay sounds like an excuse, burn it. If you do not like you, do not expect the admissions committee to like you.

### Use Humor Cautiously—Write Naturally and Sincerely

Your personal essay probably should not be humorous. Humor is difficult to write, and what strikes a high school senior as funny may be boorish or in outright bad taste to an admissions committee. A sincere, forthright presentation will have a better chance with those sitting in judgment. Read the following paragraph, imagining yourself as an underpaid, overworked college official with a headache.

*On May 16, 1958, a prize was delivered to two contestants in the game of life. Mary and Fred Williamson gave birth to a baby boy, John, who,*

*17 years later, decided to give Amherst College an opportunity to have him in their freshman class.*

This is not funny and neither is a rejected application, but many autobiographies are written in this style. If you must be humorous, have several adults read your essay and make them give you their real opinion.

### Use "I" Where Natural

The John Williamson style of writing excerpted above frequently results from a desire to avoid using "I" repetitiously or egotistically throughout the essay. While every sentence should not begin with "I," the fanatical avoidance of the first person singular leads to a stilted product. At your present stage no one expects you to be an accomplished stylist.

### Concentrate on a Few Things

Which of the following essays do you prefer? (If your answer is *B.*, then you have understood how to highlight your career.)

*A.   In my freshman year at Harry B. Thompson Junior High School I was a booster, junior cheerleader, member of the Student Council, and participated in intramural tennis, field hockey and swimming, I stayed with all these sports in my sophomore, junior and senior years and became a senior cheerleader and a member of the honor corps as well. I participated in the Red Cross drive and scholarship collection fund. I was a member of the Future Teachers of America, The Committee for Underprivileged Children, my senior class trip committee and was a junior member of the Society of Homemaking Mothers in the United Communities of Kansas.*

*B. In my freshman year I joined the* Banner, *our school newspaper. I had never written a newspaper article before and really enjoyed my work. In my later years of high school I worked my way up to news editor of the* Banner. *I also worked as a caption writer on the* Bravian, *our school yearbook. I am applying to your school of journalism so I can continue to develop the skills acquired on my high school newspaper and yearbook.*

**Use Proper Grammar and Spell Every Word Correctly—
Avoid Slang and Regional Phrases,
Do Not Abbreviate or Use Contractions**

Look at the following essays (*B.* again wins).

*A. After bunking into the coach in the halls of the high school he became aware of my size and had wanted me to participate in football. Man, that was the beginning of a three-year groove. I copped all Eastern and Division hons. and wouldn't have passed up football for all the tea in China.*

*B. I am 6'3" tall and weigh 230 pounds. When I started high school I had no intention of playing ball. One day I accidentally collided with the*

*football coach in the halls of my high school and
my career was launched. I loved playing football.
In my senior year I was awarded the Western
Kentucky State Athletic Conference Trophy for
the best halfback in the Conference. While I do
not expect to play football at the University of
Texas, if I am accepted, I shall apply the discipline and tenacity I acquired on the football field
to the study of engineering.*

### Relate Your Background to Your Future

A good essay relates past experience to your goals at
college. The ability to do this signals a stability and serious-
ness that is attractive to older people in general and to your
possible educators in particular. The crisp, simple essay of
the student who wanted to study journalism is a good example of such a tie-in.

Discuss special interests even if they are off-beat. Try,
without obvious strain, to relate them to your academic
hopes and dreams.

*I live on the California coast. The sea has always
held a great fascination for me. In my early teen
years I was a surfing fanatic. Now I would like to
devote my energies to the study and exploration
of the ocean. Someday the world's oceans may become its greatest "breadbasket." I would like to
contribute to the research for the utilization of the
ocean's resources.*

It is not necessary to claim a field of concentration to
which you will maintain undying loyalty. Even if you have

one, educators know you may well change your mind as you are exposed to new subjects. It is more important to present yourself as a "together" person.

> *No one in my family has ever attended college. Something deep down kept telling me it would be good for me. I spent all my free time working and saving for college. I've worked at several garages and the mechanics of things fascinates me. I enjoyed high school physics and am thinking of studying engineering at the University of Wyoming.*

### Tell the School Why You Want to Go There

Admissions people spend a great deal of time visiting high schools proclaiming the virtues of their college. It is to the applicant's advantage to show that he understands the unique qualities and strengths of a school, and just as important, to articulate some of the good reasons he has for wanting to attend. Have you read some work by one of the professors? Did you visit the college? Is there one department that particularly suits you?

> *My cousin Linda spent four years at Syracuse (Class of 1972) and enjoyed it immensely. When I visited her the people were warm and friendly. Linda majored in psychology and feels her education was excellent in the preparation for teaching. On my visits I attended several sessions of Professor Warden's seminar on Schools Without Walls. I have since read several articles on the open school and look forward to learning more*

*about this concept. Teaching is my career goal and the major you offer in child development and elementary education is exceptionally well suited to my interest.*

Emphasize the size of the college and the reason it appeals to you, educational philosophy, or the new science building you know they will be looking for people to use.

*I plan to be a doctor. The pre-medical program at Trinity is attractive to me. The new life-sciences building represents an ideal opportunity to have the benefit of elaborate facilities and enjoy the advantages of a small college.*

### Hit Hard (Gently)

Unfortunately, many students waste time explaining how great they are. Solid character traits and a fair level of achievement are more valuable than loud claims to brilliance. Strong points should be emphasized without offending. Sentences like "My acceptance would be the best thing you could do for yourselves" are guaranteed to bring rejection. A well-qualified individual can present himself in the poorest light with a presumptuous letter. Your record will speak for itself. Your essay should convey something more personal that will convince the college that while you are unique you are still modest.

### Do More Than Itemize

An acquaintance with 750 Law Boards and a C+ average from Brown was applying to several good law schools. His life was seemingly devoid of significant activities. His personal essay was depressing, and violated all the rules presented in this chapter. The essay had no life and no depth. It merely itemized a series of events, unimpressive as presented. In his first essay he flatly stated that he had spent a year in a machine shop. After he revised first his approach and then his essay, that section read:

> *Freshman year I worked in the Oldman's Nuclear Laboratory designing and fabricating safety equipment for a 2.2 GEV synchrocyclotron. I worked 15 hours per week and enjoyed it immensely.*

School had never been challenging for our friend until he studied Business and Constitutional Law. However, rather than merely saying, "The only subjects which ever interested me were my law courses," he ultimately said,

> *Virtually the only subjects which interested me were computer programming and my Business and Constitutional Law courses. Finally, my logic, creativity and originality were challenged. In Constitutional Law my term project involved a fully researched case then pending in the United States Supreme Court. I explained the archaic application of the pre-*Baker v. Carr *apportionment rules and decided the now famous case of* Rothstein v. State of Kansas *quite similarly to the results reached by the Supreme Court. I received an A on the project, and the spark motivating me to write this application was ignited.*

Our friend was placed on the waiting lists of two of the best law schools in the country and despite a C+ average he eventually entered one of them, which only goes to show that many points worth mentioning are worth developing.

### Have Someone Read Your Essay

Proofreading your own work is like giving yourself a nose job—you know how you want it to come out but you are too close to it to see the whole picture. An older friend or teacher can check spelling and grammar, remind you of something you have forgotten, read your positive presentation as the excuse it is, detect discrepancies you've ignored, and groan at your misplaced humor.

### Type—If Possible

A typed essay is easy to read, and if well presented, leaves the reader with at least a good opinion of your neatness. If the instructions or the form itself do not permit you to type, or if you can't type or don't have access to a typewriter, print or write very carefully. A reader who digests thirty essays a day will be turned off by illegible work. If you've taken time to prepare your essay, make it easy to read. It's your story—do it right.

# VI

# Recommendations

The basic information of your application, the auto-biographical essays, your transcript, your board scores, the interview—all are far more important than letters of recommendation. These are useful only when they demonstrate real knowledge of an applicant, relate new information, qualify deficiencies, and present well-documented praise. The typical recommendation is so bland that it passes before the committee's eye like a blank page, and officials have become accustomed to regarding these documents as pro forma and almost meaningless. This attitude has arisen because students don't know what good letters are or how to get them.

> Allow me to recommend Mary Jane Masters for admission to Boston University. She is an attractive, considerate and very pleasant girl. I have taught her French and watched her interact with her peers in The Future Teachers of America Club. She is an above-average student and one of the most cooperative and dependable members of her class.
>
> Mary is genuinely interested in elementary school teaching and possesses the sensitivity and interest to effectively teach young children. Her performance at Columbia High School and her popularity among her classmates make Mary an

excellent candidate for admission to your School of Education.

. . .

Fred Powalski came to our high school in his junior year. He had transferred from a less advanced rural high school and the difficult transition was reflected in C and D grades. Fred did not capitulate. Rather, he sought help from me, his English teacher. I worked with Fred and by June he received a B in my course and had a B— average overall.

This past summer, while working on a construction crew, Fred read ten books. When he returned to school, we discussed his reading and it was clear that he was genuinely interested in what he had read. His work still is not brilliant, but his character and interest commend him in the most profound way as a deserving candidate for admission to Wesleyan University.

These two selections are sincere, credible and favorable. The second letter, in particular, throws light on the bare facts of the application form.

Letters that consist of little more than strings of adjectives, such as "dependable," "attentive," "courteous," "considerate," "reliable," "careful" and "willing," are by and large useless. Colleges know that almost any student can find two teachers who will write a run-of-the-mill letter. In fact, a student who could not manage this might score points for being unique.

## *The Right Writers*

The most important part of the recommendation-letter procedure is your selection of the writer. This choice is often the only variable within your control. Practical judgment dictates that you choose people who know something concrete and interesting about you. Even if you received a 98 in geometry, avoid asking the geometry teacher for a recommendation if he will say little more than, "Mark is an excellent geometry student. He received a 98 in my course." Such a recommendation may diminish the effect of your high grade by implying that you were a nonentity in this teacher's class.

If your geometry teacher will write a strong recommendation, it is not helpful to ask your algebra teacher. Even MIT cringes at pyramiding praise in a single field. If the only two teachers who like you are math teachers, you're stuck with both of them, but as a general rule, seek praise from diverse sectors of your high school.

It is also helpful to obtain recommendations from someone familiar with your extracurricular activities or personal life. Testimonials to perseverance, leadership ability, and maturity are especially helpful because academic records do not reflect such information. If possible, ask the writer to emphasize a particular aspect of your background or to coordinate his recommendation with your application by elaborating on activities in which you have demonstrated some talent.

### Cultivation

Cultivate relationships that will give a teacher some insight into you as an individual and some interest in your success. While premeditated relationships may seem unattractive, there are practical benefits to be derived from friendships with teachers, if you can comfortably manage them. If you have shared an enjoyable experience with a teacher, he or she can be counted on to communicate that special information. It may be that you and your tenth-grade biology teacher really liked each other. It would be sensible, as well as fun, to keep in contact. High school teaching can be an alienating experience, and teachers welcome the opportunity to identify closely with a particular student's career.

The most important recommendation you will receive is the "school's" or "principal's" recommendation. Written by the principal, guidance counselor or college adviser, it represents the school's official evaluation of your qualifications. It frequently compares you with other current and past applicants from the school.

You can generally count on the school using its best efforts on your behalf, since college admissions help determine a principal's and a school's reputation. It is not uncommon for this recommendation to conclude with: "Central High School has many good applicants to Purdue this year, but if you are going to accept just one, it should be Robert Baker." The lesson is clear. If there is a basis for a relationship with the person who writes this evaluation, develop it. If not, attempt to get another teacher who knows you better to write that crucial school recommendation.

### Desperation Rules for Selecting Teachers

It is best to have a strong relationship with the teacher you ask to recommend you, but if, like the majority of students, you have no special relationships and are not sure where to turn, here are some suggestions:

1. English and social science teachers are generally more articulate than their math and science colleagues. It is better to be described as

> . . . a young man who displays a sensitivity towards his studies and literary insight. In an assignment to re-create the ending of a popular 20th-century novel, the closing lines Billy gave to *The Great Gatsby* were nearly worthy of Mr. Fitzgerald himself. Billy demonstrated a feeling for literature not at all reflected in his grades.

than:

> Billy was in my 11th-grade chemistry course. First semester he received a B— and in June he received a B. This placed him in the 60% percentile, which is 10% above the mean. His performance was variable but his standard deviation was never more than the coefficient of variation in the class. Lab performance was graded less rigorously but he ranked 13th out of the 27 students in his section. His lab instructor described him as "neat."

2. Other things being equally uncertain, go to the teacher who gave you the highest grade or to the teacher in whose

class you were a positive standout, either in terms of grades, class participation or informal discussion with the teacher after class. For example, one student with an 82 in trig was recommended with high praise for his overall academic potential and athletic abilities. The student ran a very fast 100-yard dash and his trigonometry teacher was also his track coach.

3. Look to your younger teachers. Many older teachers have tired of writing recommendations year after year. These teachers produce letters of recommendation which can look like this:

> MORTIMER OLINSKY        is an excellent candidate for        OREGON STATE UNIVERSITY      . He  (she)  has demonstrated his (her) ability in advanced placement history and I am sure he  (she)  will succeed at OREGON STATE UNIVERSITY        .

If you think a teacher will merely fill in the blanks on a form (either in his mind or on paper) you should ask another.

4. Go to the softees, but only if you're having trouble. Some teachers write good recommendations for everyone, whether because they abhor the entire process, are too lazy to evaluate each student, or want all their students to do well. However, bear in mind that the letters of such faculty members may be "soft" too, and they should be used only as a last resort.

5. Avoid the most popular teachers. Unfortunately, some teachers who are well known and who in turn know many students well, are swamped yearly with requests for rec-

ommendations. If a teacher is asked to write fifty or sixty letters, he can't take the time and care to write a full helpful report. If you have a choice, go to the teacher who can do the best job for you.

### Respected, Rich or Famous People

Should you request a well-known individual to write a letter on your behalf? If you can get the President of the United States or the president of the university to write a letter for you, do it. Such a letter surely will be helpful. A senator may help a bit if you are so tied in with him that his position, power and relationship to you add to your attractiveness. Don't bother others like congressmen, priests or millionaires unless by their recommendation the university will be made to see a decided benefit from accepting you. If the writer will give money or can endorse your skills in his field or has political power that touches the university, his recommendation will be meaningful. A Kentucky congressman sending a letter of recommendation to a Massachusetts university, a millionaire alumnus of Swarthmore recommending his nephew to Williams, a symphony conductor recommending a geology candidate—all are wasting their time.

### Alumni

The fact that you are a child of an alumnus can help and never hurt. However, mentioning the relationship is sufficient. Nothing stretches credibility like a father's wholehearted endorsement of his son. Letters of recommendation from parents should not be sent.

Alumni letters that are the product of friendship or

obligation should generally be avoided. Unless you know that the individual will write a meaningful letter or that the college actively seeks alumni endorsement, do not bother your parents' friends.

### Unsolicited Accolades

Colleges make explicit the number of recommendations they want. In all but extreme cases this restriction should be scrupulously respected. Only when you have the recommendation of an individual of great influence should an unsolicited letter be sent.

The people who make admissions decisions are flooded with information and influences. Though they recognize and respond to significant pressures, unjustified pushing is simply annoying and likely to produce an adverse reaction. While unsolicited recommendations are politely and routinely acknowledged, admissions officers will assume that the applicant is either unable or unwilling to follow instructions.

### Unexpected Disaster

Paul Shmidling has for some reason beyond my comprehension asked me to write a letter of recommendation on his behalf. A college might overlook his miserable conduct and belligerent attitude, but you cannot ignore that he is almost certain to drop out after four months due to his instability and super-adolescent neuroses. Paul is likely to do a lot at college. He will organize the athletes to strike for more financial assistance and assist the cheerleaders by arranging dates with local businessmen at fifty bucks a throw. His

despicable and basically immoral nature can recommend Paul highly to one place—and they
don't graduate from down there.

While a mildly favorable recommendation may not count
for much, a bad one can be disastrous. Teachers are human
and some are unfortunately more human than others.
Hidden prejudices and old grudges can surface at this the
worst of times. Most teachers will have you ask someone
else rather than seize the opportunity to destroy you. Another more likely possibility is that a teacher, too embarrassed to tell you that he has nothing to say, will agree to
write a recommendation, which turns out so weak as to be
negative.

Unless you have absolute favorites whom you can trust,
do not use the same teachers to write all your recommendations. If five of your teachers like you, ask different ones
to write to different schools. This will prevent mysterious
across-the-board rejections.

We should note here that inexplicable rejection is by no
means always the fault of an unexpected guillotine letter.
The majority of high school teachers deserve the highest
praise for donating their time year after year and diligently
helping students get into college.

### Padding the Bill

Frequently when you ask someone to write a recommendation, he will ask you to write a prototype letter for him
to modify. This is helpful to both the writer and you. Neatly
type a brief recommendation, following the general principles for good autobiography and recommendation. Include

the salient points which will be most impressive coming from this person and briefly state them in an enthusiastic endorsement. This is no time for modesty. Present the writer with a finished product he could be proud to call his own work. If he likes it, he will send it as is. In fact, if the writer doesn't ask for any material from you, you might offer to write a brief letter or a summary sketch of your background. If he plans to write a long letter, at least furnish him with meaningful material he can use.

Your sketch can present those of your attributes to which the writer can relate. The track coach should not be given an outline emphasizing your physics grades, and your English teacher should not have to write about your athletic prowess. Your employer should write about your job performance and your guitar teacher about your musical talent.

Recommendations should not be ridiculously praiseworthy. Avoid a credibility gap. Great recommendations require a great story. There are few stories like the polio victim who became an all-state place kicker. You are more likely to be the C+ student who worked thirty hours a week to support his ailing parents. Get a letter from the gas-station owner in praise of the thirty hours a week, and a letter from your guidance counselor describing your determination in school despite problems at home.

## *Summary*

Letters of recommendation are, as we have seen, of dubious impact. They become important only if they're bad. To get the best letter possible:

1. The letter should show a real knowledge of you, relate new information, qualify deficiencies and present well-documented praise.
2. Choose people who know something concrete and interesting about you which is not readily discernible from your application.
3. Seek people from diverse sectors of your life.
4. If you lack a clear-cut choice of a high school teacher, remember
   a. English and social science teachers are generally more articulate than their science and math colleagues.
   b. Ask teachers in whose courses you performed the best.
   c. Look to younger teachers.
5. Guard against mysterious disaster by requesting different teachers to write your recommendations for various colleges.
6. Ask the writer to be brief.
7. When asked to supply your background information choose the salient points which will be most impressive coming from the particular person. Avoid false modesty.
8. Supply the writer with material that is positive but balanced. Recommendations should be believable.

# VII
## The
## Interview

Not all colleges require a personal interview, a time-consuming process that requires advance planning and extra effort. If you're going to apply only to large state schools, you probably can skip this chapter. However, if a school does want to interview you, consider yourself lucky, for if you handle it well, you add a further dimension—hopefully a positive one—to your application effort.

Understand your interviewer and make him like you. Tell him about yourself, maximizing that aspect he is likely to approve. Don't ask a lot of questions about the school in an effort to appear bright-eyed and eager. Follow his lead, responding fully when he asks a leading question, answering succinctly when he's just trying to clarify a point of information.

Each neophyte reacts in his own way to the pressure of the interview, one with misplaced confidence, another with temporary muteness, another with awkward honesty.

Paul, for example, let his anxieties get the best of him.

Interviewer:   How do you like your high school?

Paul:   It is very fine but I welcome the greater challenge of college that awaits, sir! I would like to discuss my painting.

Interviewer:   Go right ahead.

Paul:          I study under Pierre Seral, a very fine painter. You may have seen his work. Have you?

Interviewer:   No.

Paul:          Well, he is really an exceptional post-impressionist painter and does fine sculpture.

Interviewer:   That sounds very nice. I assume you paint well.

Paul:          Yes, sir.

Interviewer:   And you enjoy it?

Paul:          Very much.

Interviewer:   Why would you like to come to the University of Chicago?

Paul:          Did you go to Chicago?

Interviewer:   Yes.

Paul:          Well, it's a very fine school and of course, Father went there. It's been an expectation that I would go to Chicago. The family has always encouraged any academic pursuits and getting into the best, i.e., Chicago represents a kind of victory, you know, in keeping with being the best.

Interviewer:   These hardly seem like good reasons for choosing a college.

Paul:   They are not my only reasons. Mostly I would like to go to Chicago because of the exciting student body and the good academic atmosphere.

Paul was a first-rate applicant—poised and articulate in most situations—but at this crucial moment he could not control his responses and his desire to impress. He elaborated when a short answer was preferable, and was brief when he should have expressed his ideas and feelings more fully. Paul was rejected despite high boards and good grades.

Here is a list of common interview pitfalls and the resultant don'ts:

**Don't** give staccato answers about how good you are. Without bragging, explain your talents and accomplishments.

**Don't** give one-word answers about what you enjoy. Explain why particular things interest you.

**Don't** ask the interviewer awkward questions about his job or his background. Don't assume he hasn't done a certain thing. (One young man who was being interviewed by an alumnus who was a professional football player said, "I don't know if you've ever played varsity sports, but . . .")

Appreciate the interviewer's humor. A timely and sincere chuckle will demonstrate your good taste.

**Don't** try to impress the interviewer with your family or friends.

**Don't** be clumsily honest. Many people want to go to college to get ahead, make money, gain status or satisfy their family, but those are not reasons that will favorably impress your interviewer.

Try not to go to the interview without first looking around the campus and learning something about it.

**Don't** limit what you tell the interviewer to things the application contains. Elaborate where useful.

Avoid hip talk and don't use the phrase "you know." If he does know, there's no need to tell him, and if he doesn't, he'll be insulted.

**Don't** say you like the college because someone else likes it. Get your reasons together beforehand—the courses offered, flexibility, challenge, location, social life.

**Don't** say you don't enjoy reading: college requires prodigious amounts of reading.

Avoid comments about the school's capricious admissions policy. Many people are tempted to complain about the applicant with excellent grades who was rejected, while a guy with an influential father was admitted. If it's true, you can be sure nobody is proud of it, and if it's not, you sound foolish.

Volunteering the information that you have used drugs may be honest, but it may also lead to your rejection. However, if a young interviewer pointedly asks if you've tried marijuana, a qualified yes may be advisable. Be direct with your answer, but do not admit to more than a trial, and express concern about drug abuse. Knowledge will not imply dependence and those who pretend total ignorance will seem phony or just unaware.

If the interviewer asks about your social life, tell him you date. Do not discourse on your sex life.

Riots, bombings and killings have made colleges wary of political activists. Your own judgment will dictate the way to discuss your role as organizer of a sit-in or editor of a radical newspaper. A moderate approach, adopted for its expedience, would be to express these activities in a positive manner, saying you want to raise the economic condition of the "Other America," not destroy the "exploitive capital-ists." You may wish to exclude schools that reject your values, or feel that the long-term benefits from attending a certain school justify a discreet presentation. A small compromise to lesser minds today could give you the oppor-tunity to vindicate your values tomorrow.

This initial advice has been phrased in terms of don'ts because students sometimes jump into interviews with an uninformed and overenthusiastic desire to please which can spoil everything. Prepare, then relax and be the real you, probably a little nervous, but ready and able to make a positive presentation.

## *The Adversary*

A good interview counts heavily in your favor and can compensate for inadequacies on paper. The key to inter-view success is to understand first who your interviewer is and then how to make him understand you.

In many cases the interviewer is quite confident of his ability to evaluate others, and therein lies his vulnerability.

Interviewers, rightly or wrongly, often have lost respect for SAT scores, high school grades, and other people, and instead place absolute faith in their own judgment. Whether or not your interviewer has exalted notions of his own importance, knowing who he is and what he's about will be to your advantage. Interviewers can be faculty members, admissions office staff, alumni, recent graduates or current students. Interviewers span decades in age. They represent any number of political prejudices, social and economic views, and opinions on the most desirable behavior and attitudes for a young person. Usually an interviewer likes to talk, thinks he is bright and believes there is prestige in being associated with his college.

A faculty member who has the time to interview applicants for the freshman class probably thinks of his position as that of a teacher interested in his students' welfare and the university's future. Indicate, implicitly or explicitly, that you want a college that values teaching, not only research, where professors are interested in the students. When faculty members raise their voices in support of an applicant, they are heard. After the interview, thank Professor Klinghoffer, and shake his hand.

To impress admissions staff people favorably you must take a somewhat different approach than with a faculty member. If the interviewer's hair is neat, his shirt striped and his wall decorated with college mementos, you should shake hands firmly, say it's good to meet him, sit down crisply and look wide-eyed. He will ask you how you like the college and you should respond with a prompt and specific affirmation about the beauty of the campus, the vitality, the academic facilities and the athletic program.

Admissions people are affable. They must be effective in influencing the best students to apply. They must convey good will, cheer and optimism to the alumni they meet. And they must proudly but fondly remain within the good graces of guidance counselors and principals. Likewise, you should demonstrate what a good well-rounded person you are, that you are a potential leader who feels it is important to develop friendships in college. Talk college, not academics.

While it is usually not advisable, this is one case in which it's wise to ask questions about the school, since a staff person specializes in the answers and this is his chance to sound well informed.

Many colleges require an interview with an alumnus, either instead of or in addition to a campus interview. Alumni vary so greatly that it is difficult to give specific advice on all of the types you may meet in your interview. They range from fine men interested in education to immature megalomaniacs, to bores determined to keep the wrong people out. Tread lightly at first, looking for clues to the alumnus' identity. If there are good books on his shelves, do the academic thing. For the power-hungry type —who will reveal himself with a statement like, "So you think you're good enough to go to Princeton"—be respectful: bend, but never break. Act intimidated and impressed, but answer directly. Let him know you realize that your meeting with him is important and that it is difficult to get into Princeton. However, don't shower the school with praise; even a dolt can recognize an obsequious kid. At less prestigious schools, say "I'm not interested in a name, but in getting a good education."

Alumni favor well-groomed people. They have been known to write, "Mr. Brown was a respectful young man. His hair was an appropriate length and he was nicely dressed. I enjoyed our chat and strongly recommend his admission. Oberlin needs more young men like Mr. Brown."

An alumnus rarely knows much that's current about the college, so don't embarrass him with a lot of questions. Just wait, he'll tell you everything he knows. And it may very well be wrong, so be prepared to ignore it. However, don't discount this interview—a bad showing could mean rejection. Where do you think endowment funds come from?

If you draw a very recent graduate or a current student as an interviewer, and if you're really good, then you have lucked out because this interviewer will see it. If you're not good, you're in trouble. Don't think you can play on the interviewer's youth or inexperience—as young as he is, you're younger still. Relax and try to be competent. When he lures you into discussing Vonnegut or Kesey, he'll slaughter you, so discuss, let him beat you, but make points which will let him recommend you after his ego trip. If he quizzes you about drugs, be cautiously honest because he knows.

One other variety of interviewer is popular in admissions folklore, but luckily is not too common—the "sadists," or as they would have it, the "pressure interviewers." Interviewers have been known to ask applicants to open nailed-down windows, to ignore applicants when they arrive or to go to great lengths to embarrass them. Should the interviewer offer you his bandaged hand, just shake gently and say you hope that his hand heals quickly. If the interviewer ignores you, ask a question. Intelligent questions are excellent silence breakers. An awareness of purposely created tension will make you better able to handle it.

## Approach and Technique

In general, the interview is a low-key, pleasant conversation intended to convey an idea of your personality, maturity, articulateness, and ability to reason on the spot. If it is optional, assess the impression you make on people. If you feel you will interview well, take this opportunity to make a favorable impression, but if you think you will lose ground, avoid it.

If time and economics permit, visit the school for your interview. Some colleges provide meals and a place to stay for a short visit, which can be fun. More important, as we have discussed, it's a good idea to have a firsthand acquaintance, however brief, with a place where you may spend four years and thousands of dollars. Also, admissions committees interpret your visit as evidence of your interest in the school, which is good for your image.

Leave your parents at home. Having them along may generate pressure and put you on edge for the interview. At any rate, as a prospective college freshman, you should begin to break away. Take the interview—and, if possible, the enjoyable weekend—on your own.

When you arrive, try to learn your interviewer's name, his alma mater and his job. If his secretary seems willing, ask her for the information. Don't be intimidated by her, but don't be rude. Secretaries have a direct line of communication to their bosses and can be quite influential.

As to dress and length of hair, take your cue from the nature of the institution, its reputation and your own desire to be admitted. A neat, fairly short cut will not hurt your chances anywhere, but a 1950s crew cut is hardly necessary.

If you come to your interview without jacket and tie, or a dress and stockings, and you draw an old-timer, you may be dismissed—unfairly, perhaps, but dismissed nonetheless. It is unlikely that a traditional "good" appearance will result in an especially favorable evaluation, but a poor appearance can have a strong negative effect. Remember that hair always grows in after a precautionary trim. Your appearance is your personal business, but keep your personal interests in mind.

During the interview your thoughts may be racing and your emotions may be surging, but try to keep your physical person under control. Keep your fingers out of your mouth and away from your face. Try not to shake visibly. Don't slouch, don't play with your hair, don't tap your feet. For those of you who never know what to do with your hands, keep them clasped on your lap. Several variations of keeping your hands still are possible and you should practice your most comfortable immobile position. In terms of what an interview is capable of evaluating, nothing could be more damaging than: "John was a shy, nervous young man who could not stop biting his fingernails."

Topics that are most often discussed during the interview are books you are reading outside of school, career interests, details of extracurricular activities, current events, high school education, why you want to go to college, and why this particular college. You can easily prepare responses to questions on these topics and appear bright, confident and well informed. Answers like, "I read a lot, but I don't remember any names," or, "I read *The Naked and the Dead* but don't remember the author or the main character," are damaging even to a good applicant.

Review several books you have read beyond the normal high school assignments. Become familiar with some high-toned best sellers as well as the classics educated people need to have read. Read about the career in which you express interest. If you want to be a physician, having read *Five Patients, Intern X, The Making of a Surgeon,* and a few medical texts and journals gives a feeling of conviction and depth to your interest. If you lack breadth, don't lack depth. It can be effective to have read books by professors at the college and graduates of the college or books about the college.

What you want to be or what you want to study are not nearly so important as why these are your goals. Wanting to be a doctor for prestige, or a lawyer because you enjoy talking are unimpressive motives. There are no right or wrong reasons in a matter like this, but some explanations seem more sincere, mature and well thought out than others.

It is not unusual for high school seniors and college freshmen to be interested in an academic area, such as biology or English, without having professional plans. Colleges are aware of the frequency with which fields of interest change between freshman registration and graduation, but a well-articulated career choice can be useful. To talk about it intelligently: (1) know what a profession entails in terms of training, time, kind of work; (2) relate it to your abilities and preferred life style; (3) consider the alternatives for which you are well suited and discuss your choice in relation to those alternatives; (4) try to be honest, but not at the cost of revealing that what you really want to do is "nothing."

Whatever your interests, choose an ambitious goal. If you like English, say you want to be a novelist and develop a few interesting themes with the interviewer. Aim to be a physician rather than a dentist; a professor, not a teacher; a Ph.D., not an M.A. Modesty and small thinking rarely pay off. Colleges are not looking for mediocre applicants, and universities are often cautious about rejecting a potential distinguished scholar or national leader. They certainly will not lose any sleep over rejecting someone who wants to be a low-level municipal bureaucrat. Use good sense, of course, and be able to justify your more lofty ambitions, which otherwise may be perceived as fantasy.

Conversation about your summer activities can be impressive. The spectrum of possibilities is presented in another chapter, but at the interview you should explain what you did and why it was valuable. "Well, mostly I just messed around" is a sure-fire way to ruin your chances for admission. Try to extract value from your experience.

> "I was a housepainter and it was really fun. I enjoyed the work, started and ran the business myself and earned over five hundred dollars. It also gave me time to read quite a bit and work at the youth center with the kids."

If you attended a summer school or National Science Foundation program, be prepared to discuss what you studied, the value of the living experience and the friends you made. If you traveled, discuss the trip in terms of history, cross-cultural comparisons, social and economic contrasts. An inactive summer should be described as one spent reading, working on hobbies and writing. From the university's viewpoint, there is nothing worse than a student who wastes time. The value of college depends on efficient and productive use of free time.

Extracurricular positions, even as president of the Student Council or editor of the newspaper, can look sterile unless you communicate genuine accomplishment and special meaning to you. Improving the structure of the government at school, involving the members of the fourth estate (commercial and general students), developing new courses, winning new academic freedoms and raising money for scholarships are all accomplishments worthy of elaboration in an interview. However, though the Student Council president who got permission for students to leave the lunchroom or to wear jeans to school may have been doing his job, he would be wise to discuss something more traditionally impressive at the interview. Develop perspective about your activities. Choose the most significant and develop it in terms of personal satisfaction that transcends the small high school world.

The jock often seems to have a ten-point advantage on everyone else. The whole world loves an athlete, a healthy, hard-working guy who may continue to win glory on the gridiron or perhaps become an orthopedic surgeon. If you have an athletic background, tell the interviewer about the perseverance, discipline and teamwork you learned on the field and he will melt. Remember, as a group, admissions staff interviewers are the most vigorous sports fans. "Those friendships on the team, the guys I work and play with and for—that might well have been the most valuable part of high school."

While he is thinking about what a great guy you are, tell him that your schoolwork might have suffered a bit, but not your education. Nonetheless, you may not play ball in college because you are coming here to prepare for medical school and you are not ready to risk your medical career. That's what you say if you're not a top athletic prospect and are a pretty good student. If football is your forte the interviewer cannot evaluate your potential. Simply tell him about your background, records and victories, your desire to become an integral part of Auburn's football team and your hunger for a good education.

Read the newspaper. Don't get involved in political arguments, but a well-informed discussion of current issues may help you to win a positive recommendation. It is not unusual for an aggressive interviewer to ask you about a new Cabinet appointment, or, "What do you think about XIV B?" If you don't know what XIV B is, don't hem and haw. A forthright request to be informed will be well taken. You are not expected to know everything, and some interviewers will intentionally quiz you on an obscure point to test your reaction and composure.

The interviewer may be curious about your high school and your opinion of secondary school education. Having read some books about education, such as *Compulsory Mis-*

*education, Growing Up Absurd, Death at an Early Age,* can show that you have a genuine interest in this subject and can help you articulate your own opinion more readily.

In judging your own high school, be critical but generous. Telling an interviewer that high school was miserable, the education banal, the students cretins, the teachers worse, is certain to make you appear misanthropic and malcontent, qualities that admissions people want to avoid. It is wiser to affirm and then modify.

> *"My high school was respectable academically and I spent a meaningful and happy four years there. The teachers were concerned, the students bright [this makes your performance, whatever it was, seem stronger] and many opportunities existed. However, it has its limits, and did not offer courses in [give examples] fields in which I am particularly interested. There was minimum emphasis on written expression and we did not receive enough critical evaluation of our work. Often we merely received a grade."*

If he asks, "Why college?" don't say you are going to college to get laid, see football games, find a husband, get a better job, stay out of the Army, please your parents or elevate your status. You may in fact be going for all these reasons, but few institutions could justify their existence to satisfy these needs. Answer delicately. Say that you have considered some alternatives to college and that further schooling is your choice because your immediate goal is book learning—never forget that books are the raison d'être of the university. College provides an academic environment for exploring and reflecting on the real and ethereal aspects of the universe. Career goals can then be emphasized. Interest in particular subjects, developing friendships, maturing in an intellectual and exciting environment, engaging in sports and satisfying curiosity are among the many worthy reasons for attending college.

To answer "Why this college?" you should cover areas like size and nature of the institution, departmental strengths, location, life style, and reputation in the field you're interested in. The direction of your statements should, of course, be adapted to the institution at hand. Technical colleges are not seeking free and creative spirits. Schools of business administration feel they impart something substantive, and if you are professionally inclined, indicate that you expect career preparation. Express, if possible, that you can learn something at this school that is not available at other universities. Your goals should be consistent with the role the college perceives for itself. Catalogs and other admissions information are a useful source of information on the college's self-perception and of whether you want to go there in the first place.

A somewhat thorny question is, "If accepted, will you come here?" When the school is your first choice, be direct and honest; when it isn't, be circumspect. For instance, you've applied to Stanford, Columbia, Dartmouth and Colgate, and this is your Colgate interview. Colgate is your safety school and the interviewer suspects it. He would like to protect his institution from admitting people who won't come. If you tell him Colgate is your first choice, he'll know you're either stupid or a liar, so you appeal to his prejudice. Observe:

Question:    Where else have you applied?

Answer:      Besides Colgate, Columbia, Dartmouth
             and Stanford. [Intone this in a way that
             they all come out on the same level. Don't
             list the schools in your order of preference.
             Saying "Harvard, Yale, Princeton and
             Colgate" is a dead giveaway.]

Question:    Where do you think you would go?

Answer:      That's tough. I would be happy at any of
             them, although I have reservations, and I
             guess a great deal depends on where I am
             admitted.

Question:    What kind of reservations?

Answer:      Well, Stanford is a great place, but I don't
             think my parents will send me. I liked it,
             so I applied, but my parents would vastly
             prefer I stay in the East. When I visited
             Columbia, I was really disappointed. The
             campus was awful and the college really
             lacked a sense of community. Dartmouth
             is beautiful, but it's very isolated and I've
             heard it's still preppy.

Say nothing about Colgate. The interviewer may just
think you have nothing negative to say about it.

"Who are you?" The possible permutations of questions
like this are infinite—as are the answers. Other classic
openers that let you ramble are: "What are you like?"
"What's really important to you?" "Tell me about yourself."

To an unsuspecting candidate, this is like a broadside hit with a torpedo. But if prepared, you can turn this potential disaster into triumph. Do not ask the interviewer what he means. Use this open-ended question to your advantage. Know who you are or at least who you would like the interviewer to think you are. Be brief in your response but give it substance.

Here's a good example: "I'm the product of twelve years of urban public education. It's been fun at times, interesting at others and frustrating occasionally. I like my family, enjoy my friends and am particularly interested in history and hope to be a lawyer. Up to now, running track and reading American history have been my major activities."

This statement leads the interviewer to ask about your city public schools or books or track, all of which you should be prepared to discuss. Saying "Huh, what do you mean?" or, "What do you want me to tell you?" are simple for the interviewer. They give him good cause to recommend your rejection without giving the matter further thought.

Remember to coordinate everything you say with your application, with the school you are applying to, and with your interviewer. There is no set approach to an interview because of the many variables. The best you can do is to be prepared to recognize and react to them. It is advisable to practice your interview technique before submitting to the test of reality. Several approaches to such a dry run are possible. You and your friends could interview each other or you might ask your parents to conduct a mock interview. You can obtain a higher degree of realism by requesting an interview at a nearby college to which you will not apply or by taking interviews with college representatives who visit your school. (Many colleges grant interviews before applications are submitted to help students decide whether or not to apply.)

For this trial—among the colleges you don't really want to go to—choose the most competitive available. When you schedule your *actual* interviews, arrange them in ascending order of the college's desirability to you. By the time you arrive at your first-choice school, you will be a seasoned player in the interview game. However, don't leave it for too late in the year, or the school will think you're not really interested.

How important is the interview? This is a natural question, one that plagues applicants and college admissions officers equally, but for different reasons. Often interviews have a negligible influence because an applicant's performance does not vary significantly from his other credentials. Bad interviews can be cause for rejection and really good ones can assure you of a champion on the committee. At the extremes, interviews can make the crucial difference. One bit of common sense: when you are asked to come for an interview, assume it counts and perform as well as possible. Preparation, reflection and rehearsal are ethical and useful. Be you, but be the best you you can be.

# VIII
## The SAT's, the ACT's and Achievement Tests

*How to Stop Worrying
and Love the Boards*

A college entrance examination is one of the two most significant factors in getting into college, the other being high school grades. More than fifteen hundred schools require either the Scholastic Aptitude Test (SAT) or the American College Test (ACT). What do these tests measure? The standard answer is "Intelligence" or "Aptitude."

What is intelligence? Consider Michelangelo, who would certainly rate as intelligent, as a genius. It is interesting to speculate whether his talent as a sculptor had more to do with his "verbal" aptitude or his "mathematical" aptitude. In fact, one wonders if such artistry would even be revealed, much less measured, by the college boards.

The SAT's do measure certain skills—primarily, perhaps, the ability to take the test itself. An understanding of the examination, its purpose and problems, is imperative for any student who wants to perform well.

---

This chapter was contributed to the authors by Michael Barrett, Harvard '70.

## *Historical Perspective*

"Intelligence," SAT-style, means "the ability to handle reading comprehension passages, analogies, synonyms, antonyms, sentence-completion drills and the ability to do basic arithmetic, geometry and algebra." How did man with his glorious creativity ever concoct such a perfunctory measure of himself?

The SAT is a manifestation of our computerized, homogenized, technological society. The large-scale use of aptitude tests for college admissions began in 1935, during the New Deal era which saw the rise of immense government bureaucracies, mammoth labor unions and the concept of the welfare state. After the war the country's burgeoning middle class set off in pursuit of the good life. The universities were deluged with applicants and needed efficient methods of judging them. The SAT, the "college boards," a handy tool for reducing the reality of people to figures, became increasingly important and has remained so. Because of the emphasis on standardization, traditional use of the English language and facility with numbers are deemed essential. The reading-comprehension passages do not involve criticism of their content, only a speedy and correct digestion of the information they contain. With all their faults, however, the college boards are so much a part of the application process that it is difficult to envision a college admissions system without them.

In short, the SAT's do not measure any respectable version of the concept of intelligence. So, beginning now, view the various questions on the SAT's not as a threat but as

tricks, puzzles, brain teasers and enjoyable games or—
think of the entire concept of short-answer testing as an
educational racket. Place the whole noisome mess within
the context of twentieth-century history and you're on your
way.

## Scoring the Boards

The SAT, like many of man's creations, turned as a
Frankenstein on the population it was intended to serve.
Designed to realize an exciting idea, the measure of a person's intellectual promise, the SAT instead selected the components, defined the boundaries and demanded conformity
in this promise.

Threatened by mounting public pressure, the College
Entrance Examination Board created a commission to evaluate their examination. The commission found that the SAT's
are not culture-fair, that instead they enhance the performance of those with conventional education and the
experiences and values of American middle-class culture.
The tests primarily predict whether a student will get good
grades in the standard curriculum as it is usually taught.
They do not indicate creativity, motivation, sensitivity or
eventual success. They distort the educational process by
suggesting approaches to high school studies which will
maximize SAT performance.

Recognizing the deficiencies, the College Board is exploring certain reforms. Examinations which uncover less
conventional aptitudes are being developed. The board plans
to introduce tests in the fields of music and art. It is hoped

that these examinations will truly reveal artistic talent, but one wonders if an understanding of basic principles rather than creativity will be the criterion for high scores.

## *Gamesmanship*

Certain basic rules should be followed before taking any important examination. With a test as crucial as the college boards it would be foolish, for example, to sacrifice your normal amount of sleep for last-minute cramming or a tempting night-before "break the tension" party.

1. Get a good night's sleep.

2. On the morning of the examination wake up at least an hour before the test. Arrange with a friend or your parents to call you at about 8 A.M. to make certain you get up.

3. Take a shower and eat a light breakfast emphasizing protein and carbohydrates for energy.

4. Do not eat unfamiliar foods. For example, coffee is a potent diuretic for some people, and a full bladder may reduce the time you devote to the exam.

5. Take at least three well-sharpened pencils with clean erasers, an accurate watch to pace yourself, a handkerchief, and a chocolate bar for an energy boost.

6. Arrive at the test site early. Sit in the most comfortable chair you can find and reflect calmly on the game you are about to play.

7. Read the directions with care. If there is anything you do not understand, or if you get a sudden urge to relieve yourself, raise your hand and make your statement. At a time like this, you cannot afford to be shy.

8. Before you begin to attack individual questions, survey as much of the entire exam as you are allowed. Budget your time. If individual sections have time limits, keep track of the passing minutes.

9. Take special care to understand each question thoroughly—a simple admonition that is often ignored. Watch for the qualifiers—the never's, the always's, the mostly's and the sometime's—which alter the meaning of questions.

10. Every question on the SAT is weighed equally in determining your score. Begin, therefore, by working on the problems in order, but if a particular item seems difficult, pass on to the next one. If you think you can determine the right answer with more time, mark the question in your test booklet (not on the answer sheet) for priority attention when you return.

11. It is crucial that you work quickly throughout the entire exam. Don't be lulled by the bromide that few people are expected to finish. Aim to finish! Every fifteen minutes or so, especially as you feel your mind getting clogged and heavy, push yourself mentally into working at your quickest rate. The questions at the end of the test are often as easy as those at the beginning, and you had better get there to find out.

12. About midway through the exam you may begin to feel as if your brain is atrophying. Speed and concentration may diminish drastically. Take a sixty-second break. Rest your head on your arms and think about being in love. A few moments of pure concentration on pleasant sounds or thoughts can be invigorating. Pop a cough drop or munch a candy bar.

13. Keep in mind the nature of the answer sheet. It is corrected by an electronic eye, which can be misled if you fail to follow these rules:

a. Use only the special pencil provided or called for.

b. Fill in the entire space for your answer, as illustrated below.

c. If you want to change an answer, erase the old mark thoroughly. If the electronic eye picks up two answers for the same question, you will receive no credit.

d. For the same reason, avoid making stray marks on the answer sheet.

e. Be certain to check frequently the number of the question against the number on the answer sheet. When you skip a question, make sure you skip the corresponding row on the answer sheet. If you use row 49 to record your answer to question 48, you are in trouble.

14. Distinguish between an educated guess and a hunch and utilize both.

There are five possible answers for each question. One is correct. A score on the SAT is calculated by taking the number of correct answers and subtracting one-fourth of the number of wrong answers. This is supposed to constitute a penalty against unqualified guessing. However, assume that you take the test and answer sixty questions solely by random selection. You have one chance in five of being correct in any particular instance, and probability indicates that you will wind up with a total of twelve right and forty-eight wrong answers. If one-fourth of the total number of mistakes are subtracted from your score of twelve, as a penalty for guessing, you will wind up with exactly zero. In other words, your completely wild guesses will neither help nor hurt your score. If you skip those sixty questions altogether, the odds are that you will receive the same score.

Therefore, if you have absolutely no idea of the answer there is nothing to gain or lose by guessing. Since it takes a second to mark an answer, don't waste time doing it. If you can eliminate even *one* of the five possible answers, then guess, because the odds favor you. If you eliminate *two* of the five choices for each of sixty questions and make wild stabs among the remaining choices, chances are that you would get twenty right. After being penalized one-fourth of the forty wrong answers, you would emerge with a net gain of ten correct answers on your total score. That is the advantage of educated guessing, of answering a question for which your information is considerable but not conclusive.

A hunch is a different animal. In the case of certain questions on the SAT you will be unable to narrow the selection of possible responses in any rational way. But your subconscious will form an association between the question and one of the choices and you will feel an impulse to answer. When you have a sudden intuition, a golden inspiration, a hunch, don't examine or study it; take a chance.

15. In most cases, all but one of the answers has been provided in order to lead you to error. The incorrect choices are often ones you would get if you handled the problem

by flawed logic. In the reading-comprehension section, beware of the answer appropriate for a subordinate theme when the question concerns the entire passage. In analyzing synonyms, antonyms and analogies, watch for misleading choices that match different parts of speech, or merely sound like the correct answer, or which would be correct except for a slight change in spelling. In mathematics do not fall for the answer which offers the right number but the wrong unit of measure or the correct outcome of a division process when the final step requires multiplication.

16. Never hand in the exam early. Try to save a few minutes at the end of the three hours to check your answer sheet, and return to a few problems that you could not solve earlier. No matter how exhausted you feel, use every valuable second.

## *The Verbal SAT, or Love Affair with Words*

Words are the most intriguing things in the world—besides people. They have infinite power to bring us together, drive us apart, spin us in circles. Thoughts without words would be cripples, able to get from one person to another only with great difficulty. Hopefully, you enjoy playing with words because the substance of the exam is knowledge of words. The key to success in building a good vocabulary is to read a lot beginning at three years of age. For those of you already past puberty here are some effective alternatives:

1. Read a lot, beginning now. Try to cover some worthwhile literature outside your classes. The *New York Times*

will help, good magazines are better, and sports and comics are worse.

2. Use a dictionary whenever you read. Look up words that are unfamiliar to you, and by the third or fourth encounter you will probably recognize them.

3. Buy a thesaurus and use it as a vocabulary resource.

4. Play games—like Scrabble, Anagrams or Ghost. Do crossword puzzles. Consult "Increase Your Word Power," a regular column in *Reader's Digest*. These games, puzzles and quizzes have much in common with the problems you will encounter on SAT day.

5. Obtain a comprehensive list of vocabulary words likely to appear on the SAT's. Many manuals for College Board preparation include one. Authorities who say that memorizing vocabulary is a waste of time are mistaken. If you have at least two months before the test, acquiring new words will be both an aid for the SAT's and a general source of satisfaction.

6. Study a comprehensive list of prefixes, suffixes, and roots, which is sometimes available in conventional SAT manuals.

7. Whenever you encounter an unfamiliar word, make the stranger a close acquaintance. Enter your find on a list, memorize it and review it periodically. Incorporate the term into your speech and writing, and take justifiable pleasure when its use becomes comfortable.

### Applied Vocabulary on the College Boards

Your knowledge of vocabulary is tested in several ways. Each demands a knowledge of words and a particular kind of analysis.

*Synonyms and Antonyms*

Synonyms and antonyms pose fairly straightforward tests of your knowledge of vocabulary. Most students know that these are words equal or opposite in meaning to a given word, but be careful to recognize which is requested in a particular case.

Watch for the following:

1. Beware of answers which would be correct for a word *sounding* like the word in question. Consider the synonym for INGENUOUS

   (A)  rocky     (B)  creative     (C)  devour
   (D)  naïve     (E)  skillfully

(B) sounds good, but that's because "creative" is a synonym for "ingenious." (D) is, in fact, the correct choice.

2. Take the word in question, the "anchor" word, and make a sentence with it in your mind. Remember that the proper choice must be similar to the anchor word in that

   a.  The choice must be the same part of speech. If you know that "ingenuous" is an adjective, you can eliminate "devour" and "skillfully" right away.

   b.  The choice must be animate if the anchor word is animate, and inanimate if the anchor is inanimate. In other words, if you know that the anchor word only applies to living things, you can eliminate "rocky" right away. Note that if you apply principles a. and b. to the question involving "ingenuous," you can immediately disregard three of the five possible answers, which leaves you with good odds.

   c.  The choice must be of a nature similar to that of the anchor word. Consider an antonym for STRUMPET

(A)   lake                 (B)   adolescent
(C)   athlete              (D)   artist
(E)   virgin

You may not know what a strumpet is, but if you are vaguely aware that it pertains to females rather than males, you can take a stab at "virgin" as being an antonym, and sure enough, you will be right, since a strumpet is a prostitute.

These pointers can help, but success at synonyms and antonyms boils down to knowing what words mean and what they don't mean.

*Sentence Completions*

Whereas synonym and antonym questions are easy if you can place the words in context, sentence completions explicitly require this skill.

The best answer to a sentence-completion exercise depends upon the general orientation of the passage in question. Consider the following:

> Apparently consistent with the vow of an American general to "turn Vietnam into a parking lot" if necessary to win the war, our bombs and defoliants are transposing huge chunks of once-fertile land into _____. (A) resorts (B) hospitals (C) schools (D) pacified areas (E) moonscapes.

The first three possibilities seem unlikely, but (D) makes sense to a student who is versed in world affairs and knows of our government's "pacification" program in Vietnam. However, the tone of the sentence suggests that the writer has a special meaning in mind. The general construction and the particular use of the adjective "once-fertile" makes (E), with its connotation of sterility, the most satisfactory choice.

Generally, approach sentence completions with a four-step sequence in mind.

1. Read the sentence or passage.

2. Determine if the sentence or passage projects any particular tone or viewpoint.

3. Avoid checking the possible answers until after you have devised your own filler for the blank, which might point the way to the best answer among the five.

4. Examine the five possible answers and eliminate the clearly inappropriate ones.

5. Insert the remaining choices in the blank, test each choice within the full sentence, and make your final decision.

*Analogies*

The aim of analogies is not only to test vocabulary but to measure your ability to perceive the relationships between words. Analogies are puzzles, pure and simple.

The form of analogy used on the SAT looks like this:

CIGARETTES:LAVATORY:    (A)  puffing:bathroom
  (B)  Marlboro:country    (C)  classroom:crib sheets
  (D)  alcohol:speakeasy    (E)  hands:drive-in

Consider the meanings of the first two terms, determine the relationship of the first two, and finally, choose as your answer the one pair out of five that shows the same relationship. Ideally, the correct answer in an analogy problem can be found in this way:

1. Establish the meanings of the first two terms and define their relationship placing them in a simple declarative sentence that states the connection. "Cigarettes are often smoked in the lavatory" is an example, but be as precise about the relationship as possible: "Cigarettes are often smoked in the lavatory against the rules" is much better.

2. Put each of the five following pairs into a sentence of the same structure, noting grammatical correctness and general "fit."

3. Respect the rule of parallelism. If the first two terms feature a noun–adjective sequence, the second pair must do so as well. This applies to all the parts of speech.

4. Note that the reverse of a given sequence is not acceptable. An adjective-noun sequence is not an acceptable match to a noun–adjective coupling.

Consider the sample problem in light of these rules. "Puffing is often done in the bathroom against the rules" is close enough structurally, but the first word, "puffing," is a gerund, and the second, "cigarettes," is a noun.

"Marlboro is often smoked in the country against the rules" is nonsense. Constructing simple declarative sentences often makes it clear that certain answers are nonsense, providing a sure criterion for eliminating them.

"Crib sheets are often used in the classroom against the rules" works beautifully, but "crib sheets:classroom" is the reverse of choice (C).

"Hands are often used at the drive-in against the rules" might meet all the technical requirements, but the qualification, "against the rules," constitutes too much of a subjective judgment, and your intuition should tell you that it's not the proper "fit."

Thus, you are left with "Alcohol is often used (or drunk) in the speakeasy against the rules," which makes (D) the right answer.

You will not always be able to place the first two words in a simple sentence stating their relationship. Expressing the connection between terms can be tricky and you should not panic if you must rely on your more general powers of analysis. Several of the questions will be geared to present just such difficulties. Consider:

> CIRCLE:SPHERE: (A) nut:bolt (B) square: cube (C) window:frame (D) ball:bat (E) rectangle:pyramid

The key relationship is that a sphere is a three-dimensional circle. This conceptualization can be difficult to articulate and you probably can reach choice (B) faster without putting it into words. Before dismissing the simple-sentence technique for a particular example, though, be certain that the problem is not that you haven't phrased the sentence flexibly enough.

There are many types of analogies. Sometimes the first two terms are synonyms, and their connection can be stated, "X means the same as Y."

> FINESSE:SKILL: (A) generous:parsimonious (B) svelte:skinny (C) Judaism:genuflect (D) cement:water (E) Cisco:Pancho

The answer is (B).

The relationship may be a matter of cause and effect, expressible as either "X is the cause of Y," or "Y is caused by X."

APHRODISIAC:AROUSAL: (A) walks:runs (B) Serutan:natures (C) toads:warts (D) laughter: madness (E) nervousness:perspiration

The best choice is (E).

It may be "part to the whole," expressible as "X is a part of Y," or "X belongs to the general class of Y."

BALLADS:SONGS: (A) wails:moans (B) funerals: marriages (C) mauve:colors (D) gale:storms (E) kiosks:vegetables

(C) is the best answer.

Once in a while, the College Board folks will throw you a curve. They will present analogies whose only relationship is that they rhyme or sound alike, as in "squeeze:cheese" and "wear:where."

The possibilities are limitless. A characteristic sample of relationships that have appeared on recent examinations are:

A. Purpose
   glove:ball :: hook:fish
B. Action to Object
   shoot:pistol :: drive:car
C. Object to Action
   optometrist:refracts :: dentist:drills
D. Degree
   hot:sizzling :: intelligent:genius
E. Characteristics
   books:library :: wards:hospital
F. Sequence
   start:finish :: appetizer:dessert

### Reading Ability

In addition to testing your vocabulary, the verbal boards also probe your reading ability. The preceding remarks regarding vocabulary are relevant. Reading is difficult if you do not know words.

In the last decade there has been a revolution in the field of reading technique. If you have a little money, some spare time and at least six months before the SAT's, consider studying speed reading. The ability to read faster and retain more can be an invaluable asset in terms of time and sharpness. There is controversy about how useful these courses are, but you should compare the different speed-reading services with the help of a high school adviser or a nearby college's Dean of Students office. Before undertaking a speed-reading course be aware that it requires continued practice and that the skill can be lost if unused for a lengthy period.

An inexpensive self-help alternative is a manual on improving reading skills. Some people believe it is impossible to improve your reading skills by reading a book on how to improve your reading skills. On the other hand, the few concepts involved are simple, and knowing them can enhance your performance. If you have trouble reading well or with enjoyment, do something about it now. The facts are that (a) the verbal SAT is more important than the math SAT to most college admissions committees, (b) reading ability is at least half the ball game on the verbal exam and (c) an enormous amount of reading is required at college and all through life.

*Reading Comprehension*

The reading-comprehension part of the examination is designed to gauge a student's capacity to extract central themes, factual information and reasonable implications from printed matter within a narrow limit of time.

The passages represent a broad, random sampling of some of the worst writing in print. For the most part, they consist of several turgid paragraphs dealing with a single subject, deservedly obscure, from any conceivable academic discipline.

Five questions follow each selection, and to each question there are five possible answers. The questions generally fall into one of four classes: the main theme of the passage, a subordinate theme, a logical implication of the passage, and a piece of actual detail directly included in the passage. Successful performance therefore requires reading with great concentration and a fair degree of active thought. Approach each selection in this manner:

1. Survey the material. Glance at the first sentence of each paragraph, and the concluding sentence of the passage, in order to get the central idea and a general sense of the subject.

2. Survey the questions (but not each of the possible answers).

3. Go back and read the entire selection as quickly as you can with understanding.

4. Answer each question in order.

5. In cases where the answer is not immediately apparent, eliminate the obviously wrong choices by marking the question booklet (*not* the answer sheet). Then refer to the passage to decide among the rest.

This procedure may look cumbersome, but the first two steps should take only seconds and the latter three are straightforward. The point is, do not read the entire passage without any idea of what you are being asked, and do not skim the questions without some idea of what the passage says.

Additional recommendations:

1. Keep in mind that the SAT does not require creativity. Do not overinterpret a question. About three of the four categories of questions are based on information explicitly included in the text. Any logical implication will be based on information directly included. Be literal, not imaginative.

2. Remember that a "main idea" will apply to the entire passage, not a single paragraph. Beware of answers for a subordinate rather than a central theme.

3. Pay special attention to qualifiers—*seldom, usually, often, better, worse,* and the like—which alter the precise meaning of a sentence and make the difference between partially correct (and therefore totally unacceptable) answers and correct ones.

4. Beware of dogmatic adverbs, such as *always, completely, entirely, forever, inevitable,* and *only,* which create absolute statements. Unequivocal statements, frequently offered as possible answers to questions, are usually incorrect.

There are poignant examples of questions for which the best answer, arrived at after sensitive analysis, is not necessarily the correct answer. The following example demonstrates the need to take a functional, noncreative approach to the examinations.

Select the antonym for BOURGEOIS
    (A) peasant (B) rural dweller (C) progressive
    (D) bureaucrat (E) student

The answer would be choice (A) because *bourgeois* is middle class and a traditional if not entirely accurate antonym is *peasant*. To the younger brothers and sisters of the Kent State victims, the Washington marchers and the war protesters, choice (C) might seem a reasonable alternative, but would be an error of overinterpretation. On the other hand, the fact that the "official" answer is rather simple-minded is somewhat typical of the tester's mentality.

The majority of the questions leave no room for artistic, psychological or political interpretation. Be aware of the pitfalls of overinterpretation, but do not become paranoid.

## The Math SAT, or Playing the Numbers

Numbers have become a national obsession in America, where political polls, economic statistics, birth rates and body counts serve as static and numbing descriptions of the country's crucial experiences. The schools faithfully reflect the situation and teach us, by rote and repetition, that numbers are tools, objects to serve man's purposes. In reality, numbers possess an enormous amount of inherent fascination.

Numbers and words share many qualities. Both provide basic means of putting the world in order, of dividing the chaotic flow of sensations into coherent units and messages. As a result we often employ these two means in the same way, which is why verbal and mathematical puzzles can resemble each other. Analogies, for example, are ratio and proportion problems put into word form, and ratio and proportion problems can be expressed verbally. Take the problem $5/10 = 7/x$.

> FIVE:TEN :: (A) Seven:three (B) Seven:twenty
> (C) Seven:one (D) Seven:fourteen (E) Seven:
> seventeen

The correct answer, (D), expresses the analogous relationship, the first term designating a quantity which is half of the second term.

In preparing for the SAT's, remember that both the verbal and math SAT's attempt to measure the same qualities—the ability to draw logical conclusions from given information and to perceive the relationships between objects.

The puzzles you'll find on the math SAT will resemble hundreds of problems that you have already encountered in your high school work. Nevertheless, the math SAT does feature some kinks which make it a special experience, and you should become acquainted with them.

An important rule of thumb is: *If at all possible, don't take the time to work out a problem step by step on paper.* Most of the items require sharp thinking, not complicated computations.

1. Read the question carefully and determine precisely what answer is required. Many test takers are doomed by failing to understand the question.

2. Often you will be able to handle a problem quickly in your head. Consider:

$.3\% = ?$

(A) 3/1000 (B) 3/100 (C) 1/300 (D) 3/10 (E) 1/3

The correct answer, naturally, is (A) .3% is the same as .03. And .3% is the same as .003. Finally, .003 is "three thousandths," which is written fractionally as 3/1000.

3. Try to reach the answer by using estimations along with the process of elimination. Consider:

> At a certain time there were 48 freshmen, 15 sophomores, 5 seniors, and 47 juniors at the Student Council dance. What percent of those present were seniors?

(A) 18 (B) 5.3 (C) 35 (D) 4.3 (E) 9

There were over 100 students in all, 115 to be exact, and only 5 seniors, so we know the percentage has to be under 5. (D) is the only choice which fits our estimation, the others eliminated by sound reasoning.

4. Another helpful trick is to use the plug-in procedure. Substitute each of the possible answers in the problem you are asked to solve.

If $10 = x^2 + 3x$, then one value of x is   (A) 5 (B) −5   (C) −2   (D) 3   (E) −3

It should not take long to discover that (B) solves the equation for x. Beware, however, for problems that suggest the "plug-in" method may at the same time be designed to trick students. For this equation, the answer could be 2 as well as −5 and you must be careful not to fall into the trap of ignoring the negative sign.

5. Frequently you will actually have to exert effort in order to solve the problem. In those instances, beware of these potholes.

a. Don't misread the question. Consider:

If the price of a snowmobile including a 3% sales tax is $2729.50, the amount of the tax is (A) $79.50 (B) $130.00 (C) $2650.00 (D) $83.00 (E) $2648.00

You're not going to get anywhere unless you know that the cost of the vehicle + the sales tax = the total price. Assuming you get past that, you would have to set up the equation $2729.50 = 1.03x$, where x is the cost. Solving for x, you get $2729.50/1.03 = x$. Dividing, you find that $x = $2650.00$, and you have your answer, (C). That is, if you're just not thinking. The question asks not for the original cost, but for the amount of the tax, which is $2729.50 − $2650.00 = $79.50$, choice (A).

b. Don't read the problem correctly, only to work it out one step short of the proper solution. In the previous example you could comprehend what the sales tax question calls for, only to lose your head and jump for choice (C) after completing the subtracting operation.

c. Don't spend too many of your precious seconds solving any one problem. Every question is worth the same number of points, so if you haven't the vaguest notion of what the answer might be, just keep moving. Furthermore, problems are not presented in order of increasing difficulty.

If all else fails, utilize educated guesses and hunches, as set forth in the section on gamesmanship. If you review your basic arithmetic, algebra and geometry you will do fine. If you happen to form a casual acquaintance with some of the wrinkles in the new math, such as sets, functions, and data sufficiency, it won't hurt you. But do not be overly concerned. Few of these specimens will appear and reference to a good SAT practice book should be sufficient.

## *The College Board Achievement Tests*

The Achievement Tests are one-hour examinations designed to test your store of factual knowledge and your command of a particular subject. They are given in the subjects listed below. The *Barron's* Series for College Board Achievement Test Preparation provides excellent subject and practice material and is available for the examination subjects bearing an asterisk: English Composition,* English Literature, Biology,* Chemistry,* Physics,* Standard Math Level I, Intensive Math Level II, American History and Social Studies,* European History and World Background,* French,* German,* Hebrew, Italian, Russian, Spanish,* Greek, Latin.*

Many colleges require three Achievement Tests and some specify particular exams or a certain distribution in different subjects. These exams are used as admission criteria, although not quite as widely or importantly as the SAT's. Colleges also use these tests as an aid in placing students in freshman courses and as fulfillment of certain requirements. Harvard, for instance, accepts a 560 on a foreign language achievement as satisfying the language requirement for graduation. You should consult college catalogs for the details of these requirements.

Some general considerations about achievement tests are:

1. Try not to take the College Board Achievement Tests

on the afternoon following your morning workout with the Scholastic Aptitude Tests. For example, you can take the SAT's on the March testing date and the Achievements in May or on the often-forgotten July testing date.

2. Take achievement tests at the end of the school year in which you take a particular subject. Although college boards are generally an affliction of the junior and senior years, a tenth-grade biology student is advised to take a biology achievement test at the end of the tenth grade.

3. Avoid taking tests in subjects you have been away from for some time.

4. In areas of cumulative knowledge, such as foreign languages, postpone taking your Achievements until you have had as much preparation as possible.

5. All tests are graded on a scale of 200–800 but there is considerable variation in the distribution of scores. For example, 15 percent of those who take the Math Level II exam receive 800's. Information on the distribution of scores is available in pamphlets published by the College Board and should be considered when choosing which exams to take.

6. Take examinations in your areas of competence but try for some degree of balance. It is unnecessary to take three science exams, although it is equally unwise to submit a low score in English in attempting to show you are a balanced student. If you are a math or science whiz and can do a respectable though not outstanding job in American history or another nontechnical subject, do so.

7. Every college receiving your SAT's also receives your Achievement Test scores. Weigh the consequences of having all your schools receive Achievement scores you would not

voluntarily wish to send. Cornell, for example, requires a foreign language achievement test. Your language score will then be sent to all your other schools. If you are burdened with a disastrously low score suffered to fulfill a requirement, take an extra Achievement Test to demonstrate competence in another area.

8. Achievement Tests take time, cost money and involve some anxiety. If the colleges you are applying to do not require Achievements, do not burden yourself by taking them.

9. Review the highlights of your course notes before taking an Achievement Test but do not try to relearn the details of your course. The test is given nationally and coverage tends to be superficial and broad. Rather than dwelling on what you have previously studied, read a general text or review book.

Many secondary schools advise their students to take the SAT's early in their junior year, as a dry run. Others follow the more traditional method of suggesting the Preliminary Scholastic Aptitude Test (PSAT), a mini-SAT that lasts two rather than three hours and is scored on a range of 20–80 instead of 200–800. It serves as a valuable practice run as well as the basis of several national scholarship programs. No matter which test you begin with, take the boards at least twice. Confidence and experience with these aptitude tests can make a substantial difference on the last performance in your senior year, the one to which colleges attach overriding importance.

Preventing colleges from obtaining your low test scores is not a viable tactic. Schools receive your last three SAT scores and your last three Achievement Test scores. You would have to take an examination four times in order to bury the first score. This expensive, time-consuming repetition would require difficult advance planning in view of the limited number of test dates. In any event colleges discount a low first score when subsequently presented with higher scores.

The College Board people maintain a permanent microfilm record of all scores, so you can call on them for an official copy of your scores at any time in the future.

There is one way of preventing a bad performance from haunting you. If immediately after taking the exam you notify the College Entrance Examination Board that you were ill or suffering emotional strain because of a grave family emergency, they will not grade your examination. Do not expect to kill off your entire family as you regularly develop the post-exam queasies, but this method is good for a one-time eradication of a questionable performance.

The most authoritative introduction to the kind of questions you will confront on the SAT's is available from the College Board people. The Bulletin of Information which contains specific information about applying for and taking the tests and a booklet entitled *Your College Board Scores* can be obtained from your high school or by writing to

> College Entrance Examination Board
> c/o Educational Testing Service
> Box 592
> Princeton, New Jersey

Two other pamphlets entitled *A Description of the College Board SAT* and *A Description of the Achievement Tests* are available free at your school or for fifty cents a copy by writing to the same address. These are brief and useful references that should be secured at the earliest date.

## How Not to Stop Worrying—
## College Board Courses

At one time or another you may consider taking a College Board preparation course. Don't. These courses cost time and money and are a waste of both.

There is no correlation between taking the courses and improving your board scores. A rise in score by a friend who took the course could indicate a year's maturity, better health, stronger desire to concentrate or better application of gamesmanship. The same individual practicing on his own might have raised his scores even higher had he spent the course hours studying on his own. To some extent the courses force you to develop skills in manipulating the puzzles of the college boards. But they are no more helpful than practicing on your own. The trustees of the College Entrance Examination Board have studied the effectiveness of college board coaching and concluded that these sources do "not yield gains in scores large enough to affect decisions made by colleges with respect to the admission of students."

Therefore, only if you are absolutely incapable of applying yourself outside of a regimented classroom environment should you consider taking the course. In that event investigate the credentials of the individuals giving the course. There are many fly-by-night operations set up by local high school teachers whose only qualification is a passing familiarity with *Barron's*.

# *The Key*

The single most important prerequisite for good performance on the SAT's is: *know each type of problem and how to solve it!* It is as valuable to know the procedure for solving analogies, synonyms or completion problems as to know the meaning of "meretricious," "prurient" or other college-boards-type words.

The substance of the verbal exam is words and their meanings, and the substance of the math exam is numbers and their relations. In the verbal test you will encounter both the substance and problem solving, while the math exam will almost exclusively challenge your problem-solving ability. You should review your basic arithmetic, algebra and geometry formulae. Although at the time of the examination you are provided with a list of basic formulae you should know how to manipulate pi times the radius squared. Almost all of your time in preparing for the math problems should be spent working sample problems. In practicing for the verbal sections, since you will probably understand the types of problems quickly, you should spend time mastering the meaning of words.

### Practice Books

Problems and puzzles identical with those you will encounter on the SAT's are available in a variety of College Board preparation manuals. The most authoritative material available is that published by the College Entrance Examination Board. Obtain their practice material.

Other satisfactory manuals follow, in our order of preference: *College Entrance Reviews: in English Aptitude* and *College Entrance Reviews: in Mathematics Aptitude,* both published by Educators Publishing Service (EPS); *Succeeding in College Entrance Tests,* from Oxford Book Company; *College Entrance Examinations,* from Barnes and Noble, Inc.; *How to Prepare for College Entrance Examinations, Mathematics Workbook for College Entrance Examinations,* and *Verbal Aptitude Workbook for College Entrance Examinations,* from Barron's Educational Series, Inc.; and *Practice for Scholastic Aptitude Tests* and *The Complete Study Guide for Scoring High on Scholastic Aptitude Test,* from Arco Publishing Company.

Unfortunately, most of the preparation books neglect to supplement the practice material with adequate commentary. There is an obvious need for a really competent preparation manual. Until one is available, the EPS publications provide the best overall assistance.

The quality of any manual can be judged by the number of examples and the similarity of the manual material to the real exam. In this limited respect some of the material used in College Board coach courses can be helpful. One enterprising coach holds post-exam parties where he pumps former students for the most recent examination questions. The material from years of such prodding can be enormously useful and should be read if available.

It is vital to obtain at least one preparation manual and spend time working problems until methods of analysis become reflex responses for your mind. The earlier section of this chapter presents guidelines for solving these puzzles effectively and enjoyably. But there are no universal formulae and there is no substitute for familiarity with the wide variety of questions that will appear on the boards.

## *After the Boards*

SAT scores are the most standardized measure of your academic potential available to the colleges. All applicants take the same basic examination and are compared on a standard scale. Some schools ignore cultural, economic and creative considerations and set minimum standards; in these cases, an SAT score below the minimum means automatic rejection. Fortunately, most schools are more flexible. They suggest a preferred range. College catalogs and a variety of manuals describe the attitudes and requirements and the approach to board scores of individual institutions. Don't rely exclusively on the little booklet put out by the College Board.

If a school states that its average board score is 550, most of its students probably cluster within 50 points of 550. Engineering, technical or liberal arts schools looking for mathematicians will not emphasize the verbal SAT's, and a math score of 700 may offset a verbal 400. The importance of your boards relates closely to your interests and the viewpoint of a particular college. Cooper Union, Tufts School of Art and Rhode Island School of Design, for example, react much more favorably to an impressive portfolio than to high SAT scores. Bowdoin College in Maine has abandoned the boards altogether. Beaver College in Pennsylvania has made them optional. More institutions will soon follow suit or at least relegate board scores to a place of lesser importance. Many universities are questioning the value of the college boards and are receptive to compensating credentials like good grades, outstanding talents or unique experiences.

Since most schools still rely on the boards to some degree, you should use your scores to the best advantage. A C+ student with 400 boards usually will not be accepted by a school which customarily takes B students with 500 boards. Unless you demonstrate an offsetting gift or accomplishment, low boards with average grades will not get you into top schools. If you have a dream school and there is any possibility that you will be accepted, apply! But do not send all your applications to schools on the same level as your dream school.

You begin focusing on colleges in your junior year by taking PSAT's, preliminary exams which are a good indication of how well you will do on the SAT. By diligent study and practice you may qualify in a later test for better schools, but the scores on your PSAT's begin to define your range of opportunities. The average improvement between junior and senior performance is only 50 points, and the average improvement within the senior year is rarely significant. More realistically, your PSAT scores may suggest hard work for higher grades or perhaps requests to your teachers for compensating comments in their recommendations. Low scores may disappoint you, but at least you can begin to define your alternatives. On the other hand, have you been aiming too low in your thinking? Good scores can open new possibilities. Certain progressive schools are interested in students with high boards, despite low grades.

The SAT's (and PSAT's) do not seal your fate. They are a guide for action—hard work for better grades, emphasis on your special talents, new hopes for top-caliber schools and, in general, a realistic approach to your options. Let your board scores be a guide, not the final determinant in your choice of schools.

## The ACT's: The Test That Won the West

For many people west of the Mississippi the SAT represents an Eastern elitist measure of aptitude. Committed to developing an examination for students with different secondary school preparation, for use by colleges with fewer scholastic pretensions, the American College Testing Program emerged at the University of Iowa in 1959.

The ACT presents a battery of four forty-five-minute examinations. The English exam tests usage rather than verbal aptitude. There are no analogies, antonyms or sentence completions. It concentrates on proper grammatical construction, punctuation, word choice, and the general mechanics of written expression. The mathematics section requires a demonstration of competence in the algebraic and geometric skills taught in high school. The social-studies and natural-science reading sections are principally reading-comprehension tests that ask for some factual information.

It appears that achievement-testing dominates the ACT examination. The ACT is graded on a scale of 1–36, and the test-score report is accompanied by a student profile containing biographical information.

In theory, the ACT attempts a more complete analysis of

the individual. In practice, it is a straightforward examination of one's high school education. Preparation need not be as elaborate as for the more demanding SAT's. However, it would be helpful to review your English and math courses and practice some representative material found in ACT preparation books.

For information on the ACT's, write to American College Testing Program, Iowa City, Iowa.

# IX
## Money

### *A Lousy Investment*

"In his lifetime, the average college graduate earns $100,000 more than the average high school graduate, so financing college, though expensive, is one of the best investments you can make." How many times have you heard that? It is the standard lure, found in all financial-aid chapters. Every time something new is published, the prize goes up. Lately, to compete for your attention with your own state lottery, the figure has been put up to $250,000.

Nonsense. College is not such a hot investment, at least not on financial grounds. During the four years you are at school earning nothing, your twin brother can easily earn $40,000. For example, the average fairly unskilled worker at GM's Framingham, Massachusetts, assembly plant earns better than four dollars an hour, or about $10,000 a year if he puts in a little overtime.

Your brother has a $40,000 headstart. While you may eventually earn $250,000 more than he does, most of the difference will come in the later years of your career. Right now your brother can gain a healthy advantage by investing part of his earnings.

Furthermore, as a matter of supply and demand, wages for unskilled and semiskilled laborers seem to be rising at at least the same rate as wages for college graduates. The Bureau of Labor Statistics figures show that at the present time approximately 14 percent of the labor force are college graduates, a figure that by 1980 will rise to 17 percent. This means that 35 percent of the people entering the work force during this period—the people you'll be competing with for jobs—will have a bachelor's degree or better. As the relative number of college graduates increase, their price is likely to decline.

Another way to approach the problem, of course, is to ask whether you want to make your $10,000 as a bricklayer or an architect, a cabdriver or an urban transit specialist, a toothpaste-tube filler or a dentist. If you are not sure what will make you happiest, going to college will keep your options open.

The $250,000 bonanza is a dubious proposition and should not be used to lure high school seniors to college, though it is a very American approach to the problem. There are at least two strong nonfinancial reasons for investing in a college education. You are likely to enjoy the experience. It will do things to your head that will help you get more out of life afterwards. And this means more than money.

It's a lousy financial investment well worth making.

## *An Arm and a Leg*

You should not give too much weight to the costs of college when you decide to apply. The expensive schools often have the most money to help you through. Many sources of money are available and your family's limited income should not discourage you from applying to a school you really want. Of course, if you have serious financial problems, apply to at least one safe, inexpensive college in case you are unable to raise enough money for your first choices.

When you write for admissions material, ask for financial aid information and scholarship applications. Schools usually send a pamphlet which details fees and suggests a sample student budget. You should then draw up your own budget. The sample, while a helpful guide, is not tailored to your own circumstances and may be too conservative.

Tuition is the largest and most variable item in the budget. It can range from nothing at a local community college to $3,000 at some private colleges. Beware of information that may be out of date. Tuition can be raised faster than catalogs are updated. College guides like *Lovejoy's* and *Barron's,* though frequently revised, can fall as much as $1,000 behind. Your four-year budget had better include an allowance for stiff increases.

State schools generally charge a lower tuition than private colleges, but to take full advantage of low tuition, one must generally be a state resident. The University of Wisconsin for example, charges out-of-staters four times as much as residents.

Establishing state residency can save you money, but many states require more than short-term residence, state driver's licenses, voter registration and bank accounts. Residency must be established in good faith, and not as a transparent attempt to take advantage of the state's largesse. Do you have to graduate from a local high school? Do your parents have to pay state and local taxes? Is there a one-year family residence requirement? Find out what you need to qualify.

If you live at home, living expenses could be what they were in high school. As a college student you are able to earn more, and even after tuition, college may wind up costing you less than high school did. However, if you live at home you risk mistaking college for four more years of high school.

As between living on-campus and eating in a cafeteria on a meal contract or living off-campus and eating organic rice —estimates vary. Theoretically, you can save a little by living off-campus but if you are not careful costs can get out of hand. Many schools discourage or prohibit freshmen from living off-campus, so you will have at least a year to consider the alternatives.

Transportation to and from college can be a major expense. A fellow with an East Coast girlfriend might think twice about Oregon State: $100 in September, $200 at Christmas, $200 at Easter, and $100 in June. Youth fares and charter flights help. Hitchhiking is an answer if there is time. Otherwise, phone calls after eleven and long letters written in boring classes will have to hold you between vacations.

A car at college is a major expense and owning one can get you a chilling lack of sympathy from the financial aid office. Unless you can prove a car is a necessity, you can virtually forget scholarships and loans. Some schools go so far as to trace the license plates of cars parked around campus to catch students who do not register their vehicles with the school. A bicycle and a wealthy roommate might be the best answer.

Minor expenses can mount up, too. Check to see that your budget includes books and school supplies; health fees, athletic fees, lab fees, parking fees; library fines, parking fines; student activity fee, the cost of the yearbook, class dues, club dues, fraternity initiation fees; transportation to and from classes, to and from social life; movies, records, football tickets, frisbees; telephone, postage, and more telephone; refrigerator rental, your share of the TV; snacks, dinners out, a six-pack now and then, other depressants or stimulants; laundry, linen rental; the *Times, Newsweek, Playboy;* haircuts, cosmetics, sun-lamp bulbs; clothing and patches; a typewriter, a class ring, a stereo, a guitar; goldfish food, contributions and miscellany. Always leave a margin. If you find this itemized approach tedious, try our recommended average figure for minor expenses of $763.42 and see how you make out. Don't expect to have much fun for under $500, but $1,000 is on the high side of college comfort.

When you total everything, your budget should come out somewhere between $1,500 a year for the low end of public education and $6,000 for the high end of private education. It is difficult to spend less, and easy, but not necessary, to spend more.

## *Financial Aid Comes in Small Packages*

There is not enough financial aid to go around. It is rationed primarily on the basis of need. Before you can receive scholarships, student loans, or guaranteed jobs—the three principal forms of aid—the financial aid office will try to determine how much your parents should contribute to college costs. If your dad has a phone in his private jet, call him and break the news that he will have to pay your full college costs. If your family's income tax is less than your tuition they will not be expected to contribute much.

The nonprofit College Scholarship Service (CSS), a subsidiary of the College Entrance Examination Board, is consulted by most schools in evaluating financial need. The CSS provides guidelines to financial aid officers. The excerpts we have chosen from the CSS table suggest what families are expected to contribute to college costs. These are selections from the basic table, for uncomplicated cases: (If your family income is $2,600 a year but you happen to own a third of Wyoming, or your father's $40,000 annual income must support an artificial kidney and continuous nursing care, the financial aid officer will refer to other guidelines.)

In order to collect information about your family's financial resources the College Scholarship Service has prepared a form which you can obtain by writing to the College Entrance Examination Board, Publications Order Office, Box 592, Princeton, New Jersey 08540. This Parents' Confidential Statement (PCS) is similar to an income tax form. The CSS copies the completed PCS and sends it to the colleges you designate, charging you $3.25 for the first and $2 for each thereafter. The CSS itself does not determine scholarship awards, but does provide an analysis of your financial picture. Many schools require you to fill out their own forms as well.

Parents of a particularly desirable quarterback or a concert pianist might not have to contribute as much as the tables indicate. Many schools cannot afford to follow the CSS guidelines and parents may have to contribute more.

## Total Parents' Contribution from Net Income by Size of Family*

| Net Income (before federal tax) | *Number of Dependent Children* | | | | |
|---|---|---|---|---|---|
| | 1 | 2 | 3 | 4 | 5 |
| $ 4,625 to 4,874 | $ −60 | $ −240 | $ −360 | $ −470 | $ −500 |
| 7,625 to 7,874 | 750 | 450 | 230 | 80 | — |
| 10,625 to 10,874 | 1,470 | 1,120 | 810 | 610 | 520 |
| 15,625 to 15,874 | 3,140 | 2,490 | 1,950 | 1,600 | 1,430 |
| 20,625 to 20,874 | 5,190 | 4,520 | 3,830 | 3,270 | 2,960 |
| 25,625 to 25,874 | 7,140 | 6,480 | 5,820 | 5,270 | 4,980 |

* Selected categories from CSS guidelines for parents' annual contribution to college costs.

This table is reprinted with permission from *Manual for Financial Aid Officers, 1971 Revision,* published in Fall 1971 by the College Entrance Examination Board, New York. The table is revised annually or whenever necessary to reflect changes made in the expected parents' contribution figures.

Some parents sell off assets, move to a less expensive apartment, obtain a second mortgage on the house, borrow against life insurance, forgo the annual vacation, and even take on additional work, in order to contribute the needed funds.

Once the financial aid office determines how much your parents should contribute to your education, they try to provide a package of scholarships, student loans, and guaranteed jobs that will make up the difference. The package approach spreads limited funds as far as possible. Few students receive scholarships that alone are large enough to meet their needs.

To qualify for a financial aid package, read the brochures and send in all forms on time. Deadlines vary. Check each school. If you miss a deadline, send in the forms anyway, with a good explanation of why you're late.

### Scholarships

If you are interested in reading a long list of obscure scholarships for which you do not qualify or for which you will automatically be considered, consult *Lovejoy's* and other scholarship guides. You will read that scholarships go begging each year and that by writing four million letters you might get one. That is the white-pages approach, like reading the entire phone book to come up with a list of florists.

Out of necessity, the thousands of corporations, civic groups and foundations which provide scholarships turn to the college financial aid offices to administer their programs. Your chances of getting one of these are probably just as good with a yellow-pages approach. Send in your financial aid application. You will automatically be applying for numerous scholarships you never need research.

On the other hand, you should ask your high school guidance counselor about special opportunities for students in your locality. If you think he is too busy or inexperienced, ask the financial aid officer of a local college. There may be state funds available, such as the twenty thousand New York State scholarships awarded on the basis of a special exam.

If you have been in the military, check veterans' benefits, such as the GI Bill, which could pay all your tuition costs.

If you are not a military man but would consider becoming one, ask the local Army, Navy, and Air Force recruiters about their Reserve Officers Training Corps (ROTC) programs, which sometimes involve full scholarships.

When you take your PSAT's you automatically compete for the prestigious National Merit Scholarships.

Your parents should check with their employers and with civic groups they belong to. Sometimes large corporations, the PTA, churches, Rotary Clubs, B'nai Brith Chapters, labor unions or similar groups offer scholarship money.

If you are disabled or the child of deceased or disabled parents, check the local office of the U.S. Department of Health, Education and Welfare. You may qualify for special funds.

### Either a Borrower Or a Small Spender Be

Take student loans if you can get them. The financial fabric of society was not very sophisticated when Shakespeare wrote, "Neither a borrower nor a lender be . . ." You will repay your debt within a reasonable time after graduating and be among the millions of students repaying loans without undue hardship. (Fewer than one percent of students default on their loans.)

In a sense you have been borrowing from society all along, paying no taxes and producing nothing for the economy. It is in society's interest for you to borrow a while longer. When you do begin to contribute, your contribution will be improved, whether by higher taxes, better poetry, or a more informed vote.

The two major sources of student loans are the colleges and the banks. The colleges administer loans made under the National Defense Student Loan Program, established in 1958. The program has nothing to do with the Defense Department, but is surprisingly well funded all the same. You may borrow up to $1,000 a year as an undergraduate, depending on need. Repayment begins nine months after you receive your last degree, even if it is an advanced doctoral degree. Service in the military, VISTA and the Peace Corps defers repayment. While you are in school, no interest accrues. Thereafter, a low 3 percent is charged. Repayment stretches over ten years. A debt of $4,000 at graduation entails monthly payments of about $40, which includes interest. Almost any career would provide enough income to make such payments easy, though sculptors and anarchists might have to scrape.

The other type of student loan is made by seventeen thousand banks and credit institutions under the Guaranteed Loan Program. Interest is currently 7 percent and accrues from the day you take out the loan. If your family income is low, the government will pay the full interest while you are in school and 3 percent during the repayment period which begins after graduation. If your family income is not low, you may still be able to obtain such a loan, though you pay all the interest yourself. The banks assume no risk in making these loans, which are government-guaranteed. However, because of the low interest rate, banks view such loans as a marginally profitable community service to be held to a minimum. Persistent requests and persuasion may be necessary to win the funds of your local banker. If your family or your family's employer does a lot of business with the bank, you have a better chance.

Aside from the National Defense Student Loan Program,

the Guaranteed Loan Program, and certain state loan programs, regular bank loans may also be available to you or your parents, but these are far more expensive and usually require repayment to begin immediately. Loans from commercial credit organizations are outrageously expensive and not designed for long-term purposes like going to college.

Many schools allow payments on a quarterly or monthly basis. Others prefer that you deal with one of the private firms that specialize in such installment plans. Individual schools can recommend firms they have found to be equitable.

Two other college-financing plans are in the pioneer stage. Governor John Gilligan of Ohio has proposed that students repay the full cost of their education. As do many states, the Ohio treasury subsidizes its students attending state universities. Once the student graduates and earns over $7,000 a year Gilligan would have him begin to repay the subsidy in proportion to his earnings. Repayment would increase as one's income increased. Although the Ohio legislature voted down the proposal, it received widespread publicity that suggests it may be a preview of future legislation.

Yale has instituted a similar plan. For each $1,000 a student borrows he agrees to pay Yale .4 percent of his adjusted gross income (or a minimum of $29 for each $1,000 borrowed) for thirty-five years after graduation. Graduates can terminate their obligation early by paying back 150 percent of the loan, plus interest. Under the Yale Plan, some would end up repaying less than they had borrowed and some more, depending on their income.

Duke has a similar plan, and other schools are likely to follow. It is possible that student loans of this type could be offered by state governments or even by private institutions who see the future income of the nation's college graduates as a good investment.

## *Work*

Most college students earn money during the school year or in the summer. If you need money, the college financial aid office expects you to be willing to work. A typical expectation is that you earn $500 during the school year and $700 in the summer. Where possible, the schools provide jobs. They maintain student employment offices (SEO) with bulletin boards or card files of part-time job opportunities. Most schools also subsidize, encourage or tolerate student-run business enterprises.

The kind of jobs needy students are guaranteed are, with rare exceptions, boring. In the cafeteria you dish out food, collect trays, separate garbage, wash dishes, mop up after food riots, recycle the garbage you separated at lunch for use at dinner, and mop up after more food riots. On the dorm crew you clean the rooms, collect the trash, sanitize the toilets.

Try to get a library job if you can. Note on your financial aid application any skills, experiences, or interests that might land you this more pleasant type of work, which may get your hands dusty, but not dirty. You may learn something, you will be at the head of the line when your three hundred classmates come screaming for the two copies of last year's final exam that have been placed on reserve, and you may be able to study when things are slow.

Work can be scheduled so that it will not interfere with your classes or wrestling practice. Most jobs are designed to keep you busy ten hours a week or less. Financial aid officers do not want you to spend an undue portion of your time filling salt shakers. Experience has shown that almost anyone can afford ten hours a week without endangering his studies, and that menial work in small doses can actually be a pleasant break in the mind-muddling routine. Limiting the hours you work keeps your income below $1,725, so you pay no income tax.

At most schools you automatically apply for guaranteed jobs by applying for financial aid. But unlike the situation with scholarships and loans, there is a lot more you can do. Do not despair if you are not guaranteed a job. It may actually work out for the best. At most schools there are a variety of jobs outside the guaranteed work program that may pay more and offer more stimulation. These often go to students with little or no financial need, because once the needy students get the guaranteed jobs they don't search for something better.

Student employment is highly sensitive to downturns in the national economy and even when the economy is booming, job opportunities at Sheldon Jackson College in Sitka, Alaska, are limited. Regardless of where you and the Dow-Jones Industrials Average are, the more job applications you make and the earlier you make them, the better your prospects will be. The more hours you spend working, the more you will earn. And the more skills you have, the greater your opportunities will be.

If you develop skills while you are still in high school, you will have a better chance of finding an interesting and high-paying job, or of finding a job at all. While the "interest" of a job is difficult to measure, it is easy to measure differences in pay. Mopping floors at $1.25 an hour, you can earn $500 in 400 hours. Typing 40 words per minute for $2 an hour, you earn the same $500 in 250 hours. Typing 70 words per minute for $3 an hour—165 hours. Typing those words from shorthand in French or Ukrainian —50 hours?

The jobs requiring the highest skills are not necessarily the highest paying or even the most enjoyable. You might prefer a low-paying or no-paying job teaching disadvantaged kids fractions to a high-paying job teaching rich kids calculus. One generalization is safe: if you're willing to work and are prepared to do something people want, you have a good chance of getting a job.

### The Finger

Learn to touch-type so you do not have to look at the keys. This basic skill will be useful to you the rest of your life. If your high school offers a typing course, take it.

The many typewritten term papers colleges require will provide ample practice. Once proficient, you will be qualified for numerous jobs. The student employment office will have notices for typists, either on a steady basis or for individual jobs, like thesis typing. If jobs are in greater demand than typists, you may have to be more aggressive to find work. It is common practice to type and post three-by-five cards stating your name, phone number, and terms. It helps if the card has no typographical errors.

Know how fast you type. That is the first question prospective typists are asked. Most people do not know how fast they type and answer "Fifty words a minute." You should answer likewise unless you can really type fifty words a minute, in which case you should say, "Seventy." This etiquette has arisen because of typing tests, which are accurate gauges of how fast people type during typing tests. If you type slowly, ask to be paid by the hour; if fast, by the page. Double-spaced page rates range from 25 cents to $1, depending on the nature of the job, the quality required, the going rate in the community, and the desperation of each party.

Decent typing puts you in line for jobs that involve a lot more. Secretaries often compose the letters they type, organize filing systems, screen phone calls, arrange lunches, and handle some of the boss's more difficult problems. Attendants at the emergency desk of a health center may have to type accident reports.

Once you know how to type you know how to keypunch. The university records (financial, medical, academic) are probably on computer. So are the records of local businesses and government agencies. Millions of IBM cards must be punched each year to feed updated information into the computers. Running a keypunch is not much harder than running a typewriter, and it is more fun. There are more gadgets to play with and the machine sounds funkier. If possible, obtain formal training in keypunching while in high school. If not, you can apply for keypunching jobs anyway, explaining that you type well and pick up new skills quickly.

Learn shorthand or speed-writing. You can take expensive courses, but a Speed-Writing-Made-Easy workbook and moderate dedication might do just as well. Taking shorthand in high school would be more practical than a fourth year of Latin. Few college students have this skill.

Once you have gone this far, you may as well learn to transcribe dictation. Employers use IBM, Dictaphone, Stenorette and other recording systems to dictate their letters and memos. In fifteen minutes you can get the hang of the earphones, tapes and pedals. These machines are, after all, nothing more than the offspring of a sewing machine and a tape deck. Explain that you certainly know how to use a Dictaphone but your boss's Norelco is new to you. As he explains how to use his particular machine you will master it.

If you prefer numbers to words, learn to touch-type on an adding machine. It's easy. Bookkeeping is also easy to learn. Campus organizations and small businesses in the neighborhood will demand your services. Income tax preparation people hire college students to work part time between January and May. A little experience with adding machines and ledger books could put you first in line for such a job. You will be trained in the particulars of tax preparation. Work in the local A&P or your high school bookstore and learn to operate the cash register. Consider how many cash registers need manning in any college town.

### The Liver

Bartending is a good skill to learn. Harvard offers a course (no credit) through its SEO several times a year, charging $5 tuition and teaching the fundamentals in three evenings. There will be many colleges and local parties that want your services at $2 or $3 an hour plus tip. The tip is often what is left in the bottle. If you like people and have a strong liver, this kind of work is fun. In many states you do not have to be twenty-one to tend bar at private parties.

Parties also generate jobs for baby-sitters, piano players and bouncers. Juvenile birthday parties create a market for magicians, story-tellers, accordionists, and clowns. Rock groups play at parties and mixers. If you are good enough, join or form a group. If you are tone-deaf, organize and promote a group of musicians who would rather leave the business end to you.

Dinner parties require waiters. If you know how to tie a bow tie (clip it on) and on which side the salad goes (the left), you will be an adequate waiter. Many schools have student-waiter service in their faculty dining rooms. Local restaurants may also have openings.

### Handy?

Auto mechanics are always in demand. If you work for a pittance now and learn this skill, you will always be able to earn extra cash. If you can learn to fix cars, surely you can learn to fix bikes and cycles. Can you fix TV's? Type-writers? Refrigerators?

Carpentry, house painting, wall papering, lawn mowing, floor waxing, spring cleaning. Some require more skill than others. All are good student jobs.

Learn to operate motion picture projectors and mimeograph machines. Give haircuts at $1 each. Be a short-order cook and grill hamburgers in the student pub or at the local Chug-A-Greaseburger franchise. Get a chauffeur's license and drive a trailer truck or taxicab.

### Blood and Medicine

A number of college students earn as much as $40 a week selling their blood plasma. If it makes you feel better, give one pint free and charge for it the rest of the time. Call local hospitals for details. If you sign up as a regular donor, you will be issued an identification card that explains the needlemarks on your arm.

There are other ways to earn money while promoting the interests of medicine. You will frequently see notices for subjects for medical and psychological tests. One recently offered $200 to a freak who would submit to a month of smoking marijuana under observation. More often the tests are safer, of shorter duration and pay just a few dollars.

### Your Entire Body

There are a lot of people who will pay to learn karate. If your entire body is a lethal weapon wrapped with a brown or black ribbon, your income is assured.

How's your tennis? At the sacrifice of amateur status, you will find jobs at camps and country clubs teaching toddlers to shake hands with their rackets. Swimming? Take the Red Cross course in high school or at the Y that certifies you as a Water Safety Instructor. Bask in the summer sun as a lifeguard.

Some of the advertisements for male and female models are actually advertisements for male and female models. If you are beautiful or unusual-looking and happen to be at school in a big city, you can earn big money modeling. At other schools, art departments need live models, though these jobs are few.

Linebacker? Weight-lifter? You may not find a job coaching your sport, but you might be welcome at moving companies, construction companies and others that require brute
strength. Many require union membership. Others just want
cheap labor. The SEO bulletin board and newspaper ads are
sources of one-time moving jobs.

## A Company Man

There are student-run businesses on every campus. Sometimes they are organized as a conglomerate under the supervision of the student employment office. At other schools
they are run independently and without supervision. You
can become involved by starting one or working for one.

Starting your own business is time-consuming but
fun. It will pay handsomely in experience, though inexperience may prevent it from paying much in cash.
Working for an established business is safer, if less exciting. Take refrigerator rentals. New compact refrigerators
can be bought wholesale for $60 and rented to students for
$40 a year. They can last more than five years without main-
tenance and there is a handy profit to be made. Harvard
Student Agencies, Inc., rents six hundred a year, including
some that are more than ten years old. Student salesmen,
paid a $4 commission on each, average $250 for two weeks'
work. One student placed twenty-five refrigerators his first
night out.

A student at the University of Cincinnati started his own
refrigerator business. He expanded to neighboring schools
and developed a company worth tens of thousands of
dollars.

Unlike the refrigerator-rental business, many student enterprises require little or no investment beyond your own time and effort, but two $1.95 paperbacks are must reading for all potential moguls. *How to Succeed in Business Before Graduating* (Dan Goldenson and Peter Sandman, Collier Books) was conceived by a Princetonian who started a business that he sold for $1 million two years after graduation, and was written by the Princetonian who earned his tuition by writing *Where the Girls Are.* The other book,. *How to Earn (a Lot of) Money in College,* was written and published by Harvard Student Agencies, a $1 million student-business conglomerate. Both books were published in 1968 when student businessmen were doing extraordinarily well. Read them through recession-tinted glasses.

Most student businesses involve selling things to other students. If you are not the manager of the business, you will probably be a salesman, most often of rah-rah items or advertising space. The best rah-rah item to sell is the class ring, since it offers the highest commission. Others are beer mugs, banners, football programs, pennants, paddles, sweatshirts, sweaters, blazers, stationery, wood carvings and panties.

Most selling is done the first few weeks of school by upperclassmen who got the jobs the previous spring. You should write to the student employment office for the names and addresses of the businesses which might need your services. Magazines use "campus representatives" to sell subscriptions. You may feel better pushing *Time* than panties and you get to offer magazines at a special student subscription rate your classmates will appreciate. Publications limit the number of reps they will have at any campus, so write to their Campus Representative Departments as soon as you know what school you will attend.

Beware of companies advertising on bulletin boards or in the newspaper for campus representatives. Some are reputable, some are not. See if anyone at the student employment office has had experience with the firm and try to talk with last year's rep or the rep at a nearby school before you start handing out fliers.

Every school has a newspaper and at least a dozen other publications ranging from the conventional yearbook, desk blotter, phone book, and literary magazine to the fraternity humor rag. Editorial jobs are on a volunteer basis, but few people want to sell ads, so that job pays—by commission, of course, ranging from 10 percent to 30 percent in most cases. As you gain seniority, you will develop steady accounts and inherit others from salesmen who quit. If it is a daily student or local newspaper, you can make big money with a paper route. The turnover in these jobs is high. Apply early and your chance can come before the end of freshman year. Meanwhile, consider being a milkman or a delivery man for the student laundry or linen service.

In terms of dollar volume, the travel business is the biggest student enterprise. Few are large enough to provide more than one clerical job. Most of the work is done by an enterprising travel organizer who earns his tuition and vacation trips by filling chartered planes to Paris and other exciting parts. Make sure you're representing an established and ethical company in organizing these trips or you—and the people you've sold tickets to—can really be had.

## *Heads Columbia, Tails Bucknell*

If you are accepted by more than one school, you must make a choice. At this point finances should be a factor in your decision. Fortunately most schools do not require a commitment before they indicate the size and make-up of your financial aid package.

Check the budgets you drew up for each school. Subtract scholarships you are offered from the total cost, leaving some net amount that you and your parents will have to contribute. Although a scholarship is not guaranteed for more than one year, you can be reasonably sure it will not be drastically reduced in future years. If anything, it may be increased to offset increases in tuition. To some extent, future awards will depend on your performance, but once a school has admitted you and made an investment to help you through, you can expect it to continue to look out for your interests.

If the net cost of the school you like best for nonfinancial reasons is no greater than the net cost of the others, your decision is easy. If not, you must weigh advantages against higher cost. Higher cost means a heavier burden on your parents, more of your college experience spent filling salt shakers, and an increased debt when you graduate.

Student loans are granted on such favorable terms that assuming a larger debt should not keep you from going to the college you really prefer. Take all the student loans you can get before you start working to earn your tuition. Once you graduate you will be able to earn substantially more per hour than you can in college. Why spend 500 hours working senior year to earn what you could in 250 hours the year after graduation?

In your financial comparison, be sure to consider the job market. It may be harder for you to meet the costs of an inexpensive school in the backwoods than to meet higher costs at a school where jobs are plentiful and the wage rate is high.

If after subtracting scholarships and loans, your favorite college still costs more than your next choice, you may have to deny yourself luxuries in order to attend your first choice —luxuries like movies, dates, books, club memberships, travel, phone calls and food. Is your first choice still your first choice?

Will you have to spend more time working at your first choice? After subtracting class time, study time, and eating-washing-walking time from your 115 waking hours each week, there is not a great deal of free time left to pursue special interests. Is it better to go to the University of Pennsylvania and spend all your free time earning the high tuition or to Penn State and spend your free time freely? There is no easy answer.

# X

# Rejection
# Without Dejection

If all the schools you select fail to select you, do not panic, and certainly do not give up. There is a school for everyone: you just have to try a different approach. Every year many universities initially fail to fill their freshman class.

If you appear to be well qualified for a school that rejected you, do not be afraid of calling and asking why. Frequently transcripts and board scores get confused. We know of one girl with an A average and 700 boards who was rejected by Vassar, Wellesley and the University of Pennsylvania. The high school records of her cousin, a classmate with the same last name but poor grades, had been substituted for hers in error. A phone call straightened out the confusion.

An inquiry by your parents, an adult friend, or especially your guidance counselor, may produce surprising results. Many admissions committees have reversed themselves when persuaded they were losing a good thing. Every year the number of phone calls increases, and so far the schools have been very polite.

Ask friends, teachers or guidance counselors for suggestions and inquire at the nearest community or junior college. Even beyond the application due date some local two-year schools which accept nearly all applicants would consider an ambitious individual who was rejected from the four-year college of his choice.

There are a few emergency measures available: a publication, *Colleges with Room for Students,* may be obtained by writing to The Changing Times Reprint Service in Washington, D.C. This lists schools that might really want you. The College Admissions Assistance Center in New York City, sponsored by the Council of Higher Educational Institutions, will help you after you have been rejected through the regular channels. The College Admissions Center, in Evanston, Illinois, also will direct you to colleges anxiously trying to fill their classrooms, or help you with special problems. The Catholic College Admission and Information Center in Washington, D.C., is helpful in placing students interested in Catholic institutions.

These assistance centers serve as clearing houses for schools that haven't filled their freshman classes. Some of the schools they deal with are deservedly empty. They are not accredited, have poor facilities and are hungry for tuition. Some are commercial ventures set up to exploit anxious high school graduates. Even if you receive an acceptance from one of them, ask knowledgeable people about the school and make absolutely certain you will be going to a decent place.

The foregoing paragraphs will, hopefully, be useless to you. With planning, understanding the rules of the admissions game and then playing it skillfully, you should be spending your early spring playing the acceptance game—deciding which of the colleges that want you, you want to attend.

## About the Authors

JOEL LEVINE is a graduate of the University of Buffalo '63 and Harvard Law School '66. He served two years with the Peace Corps in Venezuela and was appointed a Reginald Heber Smith Community Lawyer Fellow practicing civil rights law. He now practices commercial law in Manhattan.

LAWRENCE MAY is a graduate of Harvard College '70 and has served as an interviewer for the Harvard College Admissions Committee. He is now studying medicine at the Harvard Medical School and teaching at the Massachusetts College of Optometry.